THE ENGAGING CHILD

Raising Children to Speak, Write, and Have Relationship Skills Beyond Technology

Maribeth Kuzmeski with Lizzie Kuzmeski

Published by:
Red Zone Publishing
100 S. Atkinson Road
Suite 116
Grayslake, IL 60030
Phone: 847-367-4066

ISBN: 978-0-9717780-3-0

Library of Congress Control Number: 2011961334

Printed in the United States of America

Because of the dynamic nature of the Internet, any web addresses or links contained in this book may have changed since publication and may no longer be valid.

A special thank you to Rich Kuzmeski and Shane Kuzmeski—the other half of our loud family dinners.

Contents

Introduction i

Part I: Traits of an Engaging Communicator **1**

Chapter 1: Relationships Are about the Other Person 3

Chapter 2: Listening Curiously: The Lost Art 25

Chapter 3: Leadership through Effective Communication . . . 51

Chapter 4: Writing Is the Foundation of Great Communication . . 79

Chapter 5: Speaking Effectively to Individuals and Groups . . 95

Chapter 6: The Quiet Child: Introversion,
Shyness, and Relationship Development 111

**Part II: The Learning Lab—Teaching Connector,
Communication, and Relationship Skills During
Everyday Interactions** **129**

Chapter 7: Teachable Moments: Your World Is a Learning Lab . . 131

**Part III: For Kids and Teens from a Teen
—by Lizzie Kuzmeski** **163**

Chapter 8: Communicating with Your Parents: Give
Them What They Want So You Get What You Want 165

Chapter 9: Creating Better Relationships
Means Understanding the Connection 183

A Call to Engage: Concluding Thoughts from Maribeth 197

About the Authors 201

Introduction

We all want to know the "secret" to a successful life—no one more so than parents. It's only natural to want to give the people you love most the best possible shot at success and happiness. Well, I don't believe there is a magic bullet that will eradicate failure and transform your life—or your children's lives—into a long series of wins. But I *do* know there's one powerful trait that opens doors, smoothes paths, and creates opportunities: the ability to engage and connect with others.

Being a connector has always paved the way to success. But back when the world was round—just a couple of decades ago, really—it was probably a "nice to have" rather than a "must have." In an ever more flat global economy, the ability to connect and engage isn't optional. It's a survival skill.

Yes, we live in a world in which anyone can do business with anyone, anywhere, anytime. And when the lines of communication are open 24/7—and business competitors aren't just across the street but on the other side of the world—it stands to reason that the *only* thing that sets individuals apart is their ability to influence, persuade, collaborate, problem solve, and conduct crucial conversations.

In other words, if you can't engage others in a meaningful way, you not only won't win the game, you won't even get a seat at the table.

Now, in light of that stark reality, I invite you to think about the way the current generation of young people (and increasingly, their parents) communicate. It may be the polar opposite of "engaging."

E-mail, smartphones, social media, and instant messaging have radically changed the way young people form and maintain relationships. Think about it: Communication is typically faceless, limited to short sound bites, and often anonymous. If you don't like someone, there's no need to work through the problem—you can just block or de-friend them.

Heck, even phone calls are becoming obsolete. Young women today no longer anxiously wait by the phone hoping for a heartfelt conversation with Mr. Right, followed by an invitation for another date. Now, they consider themselves lucky to get a fragmented text message, misspelled and uncapitalized, asking them to "hang out" (or worse, "hook up").

In my view, this lack of respect is just one example of the disturbing social changes that have come with "anonymous" communication. A rise in bullying (cyber and otherwise) is another one. People of both genders seem willing to say things in a text message or on a social network site that they would *never* say in person. They get accustomed to not being held accountable—and their threshold for disrespectful and outright cruel behaviors gradually increases.

The (really big) problem with all of this is that relationships are becoming shallow and disposable, and genuine engagement is becoming crippled. The most important skills our kids will need to survive and thrive in a world that's changing at an unprecedented speed are the very ones being neglected. They're handicapping themselves in a very real, very profound way.

Now, lest you think I'm indulging in some twenty-first century version of "These young people with their gyrating hips and that evil rock & roll music!" or "These hippie kids with their free love and long hair!" let me assure you that a generational rant is not my intention! (Besides, I'm not *that* old!) What I'm describing is far more concerning than dance moves and grooming preferences and has far more serious implications.

What's more, I'm not anti-technology—I use these tools every day, and I love the convenience, ease, and accessibility that they bring to my professional and personal life. I know the cyber-genie is out of the bottle and it's not going back in. That's okay. I just don't want technology to shape how we—and especially how our children—form and cultivate relationships. And too many parents are neglecting to help their kids balance their Facebook skills with the critical *face-to-face* skills that will help them lead happier, more successful lives.

As far as I'm concerned, here's the bottom line: The ill effects of not learning how to meaningfully and productively engage with others are very real and very destructive. Indeed, the long-term consequences may be truly crippling. That being the case, it's up to us as parents to take a proactive role in teaching our kids how to communicate with others in a genuine way. And this book is filled with practical tips for doing just that.

I'll warn you—your kids may not enjoy every aspect of their connecting education since they'll be going against the cultural grain, but I assure you that you'll be doing them a tremendous favor by counteracting what they're learning from growing up in an increasingly "connected" (yet actually deeply *dis*connected) society.

Success in Business Defined

I have had the great fortune of being able to personally meet some of the most successful business professionals in the world. Some of them are clients of my marketing consulting firm. Others are colleagues and other individuals I've met along the way—during conferences, at speaking engagements, even on airplanes.

I have long been captivated by the "how do they do it" aspect of success in business, and I know I'm not the only one who asks: How do they think? What are their characteristics? What are the similarities amongst the most successful businesspeople? What has combusted to make them who they are and to produce such exceptional accomplishments?

Introduction

In an attempt to answer these questions about profitable businesses and individuals, I have considered their intellectual power, their competitiveness, their determination, their implementation strategies, their staff, their funding options—just about anything I could think of that might have contributed to such positive results. And as you might expect, I found that most extraordinary businesspeople do possess persistence, drive, a strong work ethic, intelligence, the ability to generate new ideas, the ability to change, a 'never take no for an answer' mindset, etc.

However, I found that there is one more key characteristic that encourages and drives success: It is these individuals' particular ability to connect with others and to form meaningful relationships. All of this research led me to write a book called *The Connectors: How the World's Most Successful Businesspeople Build Relationships and Win Clients for Life* (Wiley, 2009). Its overwhelming conclusion is that **a person who has the ability to communicate effectively with others has a success-creating skill that is unrivaled by any other, including intelligence, talent, and good grades in school.**

As I researched and wrote my book, I also found that the ability to connect is not as easy to pin down as academic intelligence or having an entrepreneurial spirit. It's a different kind of intelligence—one that is the proverbial "icing on the cake" for most of the people who have achieved high levels of greatness. And without the icing, those high achievers will tell you, the cake would be missing a key ingredient, because relating in an impactful way cultivates sales, leadership power, and personal success.

Of course, life is not all business. And financial success is not the driving force behind all of my research on what makes a connector or an engaging child. The same skills that make a person successful in his or her profession also make him or her happy in general, regardless of age, interests, or occupation. And happiness is what all parents really want for their kids, even more than the proverbial corner office, prestigious title, and hefty income.

Helping Kids Connect for Life

Luckily, you don't need to be a psychologist to raise relationship-oriented kids, or to know that getting better at engaging with others takes practice. I'm certainly not one, but I *am* a mother to two teenagers. Through the years, I've used what I've learned from my clients to help my children cultivate connecting skills that they might not learn at school but that will *definitely* serve them well throughout their lives. And that's also why I've written this book: to give you the tools to help your own children hone this critical skill set.

It's true that the ability to communicate effectively comes more naturally to some than to others, but it's a skill that everyone can learn and improve upon—including children. And yet I've noticed that we have a tendency to brush off the importance of being able to connect and create relationships, which is a real shame. Engaged and engaging kids are ones who will be fulfilled and content as adults because they are successful at the things that matter most: relationships, values, and human interdependence.

You should know before you begin that you're facing something of an uphill battle. In our often self-centered society, children (and adults too) are surrounded with a "me, me, me" attitude that leaves little room for concern for others. Especially in such an environment, focusing outside oneself is a skill that must be practiced and trained. And raising children with these skills is a particular challenge in the age of faceless communications.

Fortunately, at its core, engaging with others is not an incredibly difficult skill to master. It involves focusing on others, paying attention to them, listening to them, and caring about them.

My daughter, Elizabeth, or Lizzie as she much prefers, has joined me in my effort to encourage kids to engage. (You probably noticed her name on the cover.) Lizzie is seventeen years old, and since she began to speak, she has exhibited a strong natural ability to engage and connect. She has been able to watch over what I've written and has added her feedback to make this book truly applicable to parents, children, and teens today.

Lizzie's insight has been invaluable to me throughout the writing process, but I'm most proud of the fact that she has written the third section of this book herself. Lizzie's section is aimed at her own peers, because I have learned that young adults and teens have a unique understanding of what adults say and often respond best to advice from someone within their own age group. It is our hope that you'll simply hand Section Three over to your own teen to read.

Ultimately, my daughter and I wrote this book to share what parents are doing today to prepare and teach children to have real relationships. From our own experience, we know that engaging with others (and with each other!) is a key ingredient to happiness and future success. And we hope this book will play some small role in helping you and your children grow, learn, and have a bit of fun along the journey.

Part I

Traits of an Engaging Communicator

1

Relationships Are about the Other Person

Here is a truth I believe many people miss: Communicating is *not* what you say or what you write, but how it's received by others. Yes, relationships are developed and enhanced through clear communication, but true connecting is not as much about "clear and concise" as it is about impact. You may have heard the saying "It's not what you say; it's how you say it"… and that's true, at least partially.

Ultimately, I believe that effective communication is about what you say AND how you say it, because together these factors impact the way people feel *about themselves*. That is excellent communication defined. It's all about how you make the other person feel.

The concept of focusing on the *other* person in order to develop strong relationships is a simple one in theory, but it's also much easier said than done. Making a conversation about the other person and *not* about yourself is incredibly difficult for adults to do successfully. (Think about your own social interactions. How often do you find yourself tuning out what the other person is saying as you wait anxiously for the chance to tell *your* scary flight story, to offer up *your* advice on coping with an alcoholic relative, to change the subject to what *your* family did over the weekend? Probably more often than you'd like to admit!)

In fact, overcoming this communication "barrier" is why I've written this book. I believe that since children are by their very definition growing and developing, they are in the best position of all to gain a sense of empathy as they mature. When this "it's not about me" aspect of connecting is ingrained in a person since childhood, he will forever be a master communicator.

That said, it's not exactly a piece of cake for kids to focus on others. (In fact, for many of them it's supremely difficult!) They are still developing their social intelligence as well as an accurate awareness of how they themselves feel. In other words, it's tough for young people to take into account how *other* people are thinking or feeling. Teens may have a more strongly developed sense of social intelligence, but it can often be compromised by the cocktail of judgment-clouding hormones coursing through their bodies.

The bottom line is, despite the fact that they are theoretical "blank slates," children and teens are naturally narcissistic. (This is one of the reasons why the teen years can be so challenging for parents!) Think about it: Kids leave clothes on the floor for you to pick up. They hog the bathroom for hours when they know others need to use it, too. They don't call you when they know they're going to miss curfew. They neglect writing Great-Aunt Rose a thank-you note for the birthday money she sent. If these behaviors are all too familiar, don't assume that you're a bad parent or that your child or teen is a bad person. It's just that self-centeredness is their default setting.

It's up to us as parents to counteract this natural tendency by teaching our kids the truth about connecting. First, we need to help them understand how it works: When interactions can be directed toward the other person and away from yourself, the result is the successful ability to engage. To look at things from the opposite angle, you choose to engage with another person because of the way he or she makes you feel.

> **You choose to engage with another person because of the way he or she makes you feel.**

Social Intelligence Is Your Social Radar

It may be helpful to refer to some of the research and studies that have been done on social intelligence. Columbia University psychologist Edward L. Thorndike maintained that there are three main "intelligences": abstract, mechanical, and social. In a 1930s *Harper's Magazine* article, Thorndike defined social intelligence as the ability to understand others and "act wisely in human relations." He maintained that social intelligence is different from academic ability, and that it's a key element in what makes people succeed in life.

Going into more detail, author Karl Albrecht defines social intelligence in his book *Social Intelligence: The New Science of Success*[i] as a combination of the following:

- An awareness of the feelings, needs and interests of others (sometimes called your "social radar")
- An attitude of generosity and consideration
- A set of practical skills for interacting successfully in various situations

Social intelligence, therefore, plays an important role in determining personal and professional success.

The Socially Intelligent Financial Advisor

I first witnessed dramatic results from a businessperson who was truly using his social intelligence while I was working with a financial advisor and his firm. My company was hired to help this organization improve its marketing strategies and bring on new clients. The principal in the firm measured progress by the amount of client assets his organization brought under its management. This man's ultimate goal was to grow the

i   Albrecht, Karl. *Social Intelligence: The New Science of Success*. San Francisco: Jossey-Bass, 2006.

business into a large financial services firm with hundreds of millions in money under management.

Much of my client's success, interestingly, was rooted in his fear of prospecting. He didn't want to cold call or employ similar strategies. So to avoid reaching out to people who didn't know him, he kept calling and talking and building relationships with those who had already done business with his firm.

The result was unintentional but amazing: This man's handful of clients *truly* loved him. They cared about his success; they brought him food; they sent birthday cards to his wife and his growing family of kids. And a valuable by-product of their loyalty was a stream of referrals. This advisor was only in his twenties, and he had little experience—but because of his drive and determination to stay in business and to communicate properly with his few clients, his career began to grow in a way he had not anticipated.

Today, this man's organization is one of the top financial firms in the United States. They do, in fact, manage hundreds of millions in client assets. And it was my client's ability to connect that facilitated this amazing success. My company ended up building an entire marketing system around that ability and then transferred the "star" salesman's connection techniques to his staff, where his success multiplied and multiplied.

Is it possible to build an entire multimillion-dollar business around one person's social intelligence? It seems so. Tapping into social intelligence is the best way to build a business effectively, efficiently, profitably, and quickly. And no matter what line of work your child eventually enters, being socially intelligent will supercharge her success, too.

If You're So Smart, Why Aren't You Successful?

Given this truth—and it's one I've seen played out again and again throughout my career—it's ironic that society places so much emphasis on academic success and the "intelligence" required to thrive in school. We praise kids for making straight As (and I'm not saying that we shouldn't, especially when the grades come as a result of diligent studying)—but why don't we praise them just as much for making a lot of friends, or convincing the neighbor to let them babysit, or selling an amazing number of magazine subscriptions during the band's fundraiser?

Consider, also, that our fixation on natural intelligence IQ measures have long been used to make distinctions between people; those with higher IQs are, of course, supposed to be superior to those with lower IQs. In fact, the identification of intelligence with financial success is the phenomenon that popularized the phrase "If you're so smart, why aren't you rich?"

However, the truth is that an individual's academic intelligence isn't the best predictor of success. After all, IQ "tests" merely tap an individual's capacity to:

- Follow directions
- Follow the right steps and arrive at the correct solution as defined by the person who developed the test
- Memorize history, scientific data, and other facts and concepts

The difficulty with IQ-related definitions of intelligence is that they refer to certain qualities or skills that may lead to effectiveness or limited success; yet they do not account for the specific grouping of qualities we include in social intelligence. Yes, it takes a great mental skill to score high on an IQ test. However, once you get out of the "test-taking" part of life—for most of us, upon graduating college—test-taking ability doesn't matter that much. Indeed, raw intelligence by itself won't get you very far.

Acquiring success requires a great deal of psychological smarts!

In the "real world," acquiring success requires a great deal of psychological smarts! This has always been true to a certain extent—but in an age of unlimited competition and scarce opportunity, the kind of intelligence that allows us to persuade, problem solve, and frankly, make people like us, is no longer just something that gives us an edge. It's now the price of admission.

We Are Sophisticated Beings and We Were Born to Connect

You've no doubt noticed: Some people, both kids and adults, have a special capacity to connect with others in a deep and direct way. We see this quality expressed by a child who enjoys telling stories, a performer in front of a screaming crowd, a teacher who has full control of her class, a leader who is loved by his or her subordinates, or a manager who is revered. These natural connectors are sensing and stimulating the reactions and moods of others. That's what engaging is all about!

In 1995, Harvard University-trained psychologist and *New York Times* writer Daniel Goleman published a book entitled *Emotional Intelligence*, in which he discussed the human ability "to manage our own emotions and inner potential for positive relationships." Essentially, he claimed that our emotions play a much greater role in thought, decision making, and individual success than is commonly acknowledged.

In his second book, *Social Intelligence: The New Science of Human Relationships*, Goleman increased the scope of his ideas to include human abilities to connect with one another. "We are wired to connect," Goleman says. "Neuroscience has discovered that our brain's very design makes it sociable, inexorably drawn into an intimate brain-to-brain linkup whenever we engage with another person. That neural bridge lets us affect the brain—and so the body—of everyone we interact with, just as they do us."

In other words, every interaction between people incites emotions and stimulates our nervous systems, hormones, heart rates, circulation, breathing, and the entire immune system. Goleman explains that given our socially reactive brains, we must "be wise" and also be aware of the ways in which our moods influence the biology of each life we touch.[ii]

To connect both of Goleman's concepts, social intelligence is the interpersonal part of emotional intelligence. If our brains are designed to connect with the brains of others, then all of our interactions are a two-way street. Every contact with another person causes action and reaction, much like a chattering between minds. These "mental conversations" are what allow us to build rapport, which is the basis of any effective interaction.

Ultimately, because of the way our brains are wired, other people can make us feel better, or they can make us feel worse. But they *always* make us feel.

That said, developing the part of your brain that fosters social intelligence isn't like learning ancient Greek or flying a rocket ship to the moon. It's just not that complicated. It's more like growing a lush vegetable garden in the backyard. Yes, you have to put forth the necessary effort. You have to get the seeds, plant them, water the garden, and pull some weeds—but the real work happens naturally. Quite simply, it's designed to work that way.

ii   Boyatzis, Richard, and Daniel Goleman. "Social Intelligence and the Biology of Leadership." *Harvard Business Review*, September 2008, 74-81.

Is Social Intelligence a Learnable Skill?

Here's some more good news: While some people seem to be more naturally "sociable" than others, social intelligence *is* something that can be trained on and learned. You can improve your social intelligence and translate it into becoming more engaging in your relationships. When you do, you'll find that you become dramatically more successful—and that goes for kids most especially!

Children learn social intelligence through observation and participation. Their first lessons come from experiencing how their parents—in other words, how you!—treat them. They will also observe how their parents treat others. However, just being steeped in a particular environment isn't a failsafe predictor of a child's social competence. Yes, it's important…but it's not the only factor. I know from experience that you must also take into account your child's unique personality and character traits.

> Social intelligence is something that can be trained on and learned.

I have two children who were raised in the same, very social house. The art of connection simply comes much more naturally to my daughter, Lizzie, than it does to her younger brother, Shane. And it has been this way since their births. Taking into account Shane's quieter nature, my husband and I have worked more with him on how to be aware of situations in which he should shake someone's hand, for example, or interject his thoughts—and how to do these things respectfully.

Ultimately, my husband and I have found that both children can continually become better communicators with cultivation (and the same is true for us as adults). And there are two aspects of this cultivation that I would like to highlight: practice and an emphasis on empathy.

As you might expect, practice plays a big part in helping your children to develop social intelligence. Constantly being exposed to different people and various situations will help them hone the ability to understand others' emotional and social cues, learn how and when to express emotions, and communicate with other people. That's why the second section of this book is devoted to helping you turn your child's day-to-day world into a learning lab.

But practice isn't everything. True social intelligence requires empathy. One of the biggest predictors of your child's success as a connector is not how smart she is, but how much she cares. And as you may have noticed, it's pretty hard to fake caring. Most of us have BS detectors that let us know, if only on a subconscious level, when someone is just going through the motions. That's why, in our quest to raise engaging kids, it's critical for us parents to do all we can to ensure that our children develop true empathy.

Of course, most of us want our kids to be empathetic for reasons above and beyond social intelligence. Let's face it: Caring, compassionate, tolerant people are generally happier than their cold, indifferent, intolerant counterparts. They're more successful in *all* their relationships, not just those that advance their careers. They have deeper friendships. They get invited to more parties. People want to set them up with their single acquaintances.

All that said, don't leave your child's "empathy education" to chance! I could probably write an entire book on this topic alone, but instead I will just hit the high spots.

Teaching Kids to Care: A Crash Course in Empathy Building

So how, exactly, do you go about helping your kids develop empathy and compassion? How do you teach them to take the focus off "me, me, me" and realize that others matter, too?

The best approach, I believe, is a blend of several strategies: modeling empathy yourself (easier said than done), bringing up the subject in conversation, and putting kids in situations where they're forced to consider the feelings and perspectives of other people.

Don't worry; you don't have to do something as extreme as packing your kids off on a mission trip to a third-world country. There are plenty of opportunities in everyday life to draw their attention to how other people might be feeling. (When you start focusing on this issue, you may be shocked to discover the lack of empathy in your own behavior. That's okay: Your efforts to teach your kids to care about others can do double duty by helping make you a better person as well.)

A few suggestions:

- **Whenever possible, expose kids to diverse cultures/ populations.** Empathy means being able to understand and share the feelings of others. The more kids are exposed to diverse groups of people, the more they'll realize we're all alike in the ways that matter. And, generally speaking, we don't want to hurt those who remind us of ourselves (or at least those we care about). If your kids know someone with Down syndrome, for instance, they are far less likely to use hurtful terms like "retard." And if they have a Latino or Muslim friend, they're less likely to be prejudiced toward those groups.

  I'm not suggesting you seek out a new "best friend" just because she's conveniently African-American. (That's fake, transparent, and usually off-putting!) But you can make an effort to broaden your family's social circle. If you're invited to a wedding between members of another culture or to religious services with a friend of another faith, go and take the kids. The more you say yes to opportunities that arise, the more those opportunities will multiply…and the more your kids' worldview will expand.

- **Look for ways to give "different" a name and a face.** This helps them relate to others in a more personal way. Dottie, a business associate of mine, told me a story about being in a fast food restaurant one morning with her fourteen-year-old son, Anthony. Here, in her words, is what happened:

    We were waiting in line to buy our breakfast and we noticed this homeless man sitting at a table. He was pretty ragged looking and frankly didn't smell all that great. Everyone around us seemed uncomfortable and clearly wished he would just go away. The manager (at least I assume he was the manager) told the man that since he wasn't buying anything he was going to have to leave.

    Anyway, my son happened to have $20 that he had worked really hard to earn. He went up to the man and said, "Hey, Buddy, can I buy you something to eat?" So he bought the man some breakfast and then asked if he could sit down and eat with him. (I'm not trying to make Anthony seem like a saint because he has his share of flaws—but he does have a lot of natural compassion.) So he sat down across from the man, shook his hand, and said, "My name's Anthony. What's yours?" The man replied that his name was Bo—and then he began to cry. He said, "In ten years, no one has ever asked me that question."

16

Later, when Anthony and I were talking, he asked me why I thought the man had cried. I explained to him that calling someone by name is very powerful. It forms a connection between the two of you and puts you on level footing. It showed the man that Anthony saw him not as a vagrant but as a fellow human being—and that this touched the man deeply because so few people demonstrate that kind of simple consideration.

Dottie added that ever since that day, Anthony and his brother and sisters have started viewing homeless people through the "Bo" lens. They always insist on giving them money and they always ask their name—so that they can say, "God bless you, Bill (or Stephen or John)."

That's the power of knowing someone's name. And it's why I believe parents should take every opportunity possible to help their kids connect a name and a face to those populations who most need compassion.

- **When people behave badly, help kids figure out why. (Promote understanding, not judging.)** Let's say your daughter Meghan tells you one evening that Amber, a girl in her class at school, has a hostile attitude and lately has been making disparaging remarks about Meghan's clothes. That day, in fact, she had sneered at the new blouse Meghan had been so proud of, saying, "Wow, you sure do like sparkles, don't you? Why do you always dress like a five-year-old?"

You happen to know that Amber comes from a disadvantaged family. So instead of getting angry yourself (okay, I'll admit it's tempting!), spend a few minutes helping Meghan think through why her classmate might be lashing out. Share some of your theories: Perhaps Amber feels insecure because she rarely has new clothes herself. Maybe she resents that you make good grades while she struggles academically. Maybe she's noticed that you have a lot of friends (and she doesn't) or that your family comes to school functions (and hers doesn't). Then, ask Meghan to add her own ideas.

Parents can look for these kinds of opportunities to help kids understand rather than judge. It works not only with peers but also with strangers who act rudely or make a scene in public, or maybe even lawbreakers who end up in the news. They're a good way to teach kids that people who might seem cruel or thoughtless or unfriendly or otherwise socially unacceptable are usually acting out of low self-esteem, sadness, or desperation. It's not that you're excusing or condoning the bad behavior—you're just helping kids feel compassion because of the circumstances that led to it.

◆ **Teach kids to pay attention to their environment and look for ways to help others around them.** For instance, if someone in the grocery store has a screaming toddler in her cart, let her go ahead of you. Narrate your thought process to your kids: "Look at how upset the little boy is. His mother is embarrassed and upset, too. Letting her go ahead causes us to lose only a few minutes so it's no big deal to us—but it helps her out a lot." Such everyday "teachable moments" can have a big impact on kids.

In general, teach kids to be on the lookout for ways to make others' lives easier. They can hold doors for people whose arms are full. They can give up their seat on the bus or train when an elderly person gets on. They can offer to help someone in a wheelchair reach an item on a high shelf (though do urge them to ask first and to be sensitive to cues that indicate how much assistance people with disabilities actually want).

> **In general, teach kids to be on the lookout for ways to make others' lives easier.**

Of course, there are also plenty of "at home" opportunities to teach kids to be helpful to others. Always insist that kids be considerate to other family members by taking short showers on mornings when everyone has to get ready, for instance, or by offering to do a sibling's chores the night before his big math test.

- **Encourage kids to include the excluded or ostracized.** Pretty much everyone has felt left out at one time or another. You can harness this universal emotion and use it to inspire empathy in your kids. Ask your child to tell you about a time when she felt friendless or alone in a crowd. Then, ask her to always do everything in her power to help other kids not feel this way.

For example, if a classmate is sitting alone at lunch, your child can sit beside her or invite her to join her group at the next table. Suggest a few icebreakers she can use to engage shy kids in conversation: "I really like those jeans (or shoes or bracelet or backpack). Where did you get them?"…"I noticed you wrote your book report on J.K. Rowling. Have you read all her books/seen all the movies/been to the Wizarding World of Harry Potter?"…"What's your favorite video game?"…"Do you have any pets at home?"

Obviously, make it clear to kids that you have a zero-tolerance policy for bullying in any form (this includes cyber-bullying). Talk to kids about news stories on suicides by bullied children. Explain that laughing at a cruel joke at someone else's expense or even just standing by and watching someone be bullied makes them complicit. While your child may not be able to publicly defend a bullied classmate, she can at the very least anonymously report it to a teacher.

- **Insist that they instigate tough conversations.** The natural tendency for most people is to avoid uncomfortable encounters. But forcing your child to face the tough conversations—with the bereaved at funerals, with sick people at hospitals, with someone he has offended or let down—lets him see firsthand the benefits of expressing empathy.

Let's say your child had promised to dog sit for a neighbor when she went out of town one weekend. But she didn't write the plans on her calendar, forgot about her promise, and made another commitment that she couldn't get out of. That meant that at the last minute, the neighbor had to scramble around to find alternate arrangements. In this case you would insist that your child go to the neighbor and apologize. Work with her to develop some key words ahead of time:

"Mrs. Nelson, I am so sorry that I let you down. I know it looks like I am irresponsible or that I just don't care. I really just forgot, but I should have written it down on my calendar the minute I promised you. I know how much you love Fluffy and you may have been worried about her while you were on your trip. I am really sorry, because I know you work hard and deserve to enjoy your vacations. Please accept this box of gourmet dog biscuits as my apology to you and Fluffy."

This will force the child to think through the consequences of her thoughtlessness and see how it impacted the neighbor in a very real way. Hopefully, the neighbor will be touched and grateful for this heartfelt apology—which, in turn, will allow the child to see how it feels to be the recipient of forgiveness (which is, itself, a form of empathy).

- **Help kids find a way to "give back."** If you are reading this book, chances are good that your children are deeply privileged—at least compared to much of the world. Insisting that they help others who are less fortunate is an important part of their empathy education. Whether they work on a church fundraising team for hungry kids overseas, volunteer one weekend a month for an equine therapy group, or regularly mow the lawn for a housebound neighbor, they're learning firsthand the joys of helping others.

  Just make sure that your children's charitable activities are not easy, token efforts. They should require a healthy amount of free time on your kids' parts. If there is no real sacrifice, there will be no real emotional impact. The idea is to force your children to put the wellbeing of others ahead of their own momentary comfort levels.

Cultivating empathy is about helping your child develop compassion, tolerance, understanding, empathy, and patience. I am not saying it is easy! In fact, we are still working on this in our family—and maybe always will. We have four strong-willed people under our roof (and it also seems that we have cultivated two strong-willed dogs). It's not by accident that we are all very similar. That makes the development of compassion and understanding an area to which we must return on a regular basis—but we do it because we know it is worth the effort!

2

Listening Curiously: The Lost Art

Being a good listener brings with it enormous advantages. Good listeners are good learners, good business leaders (or good employers), good friends, and yes, good connectors.

On the other hand, poor listeners are at a distinct *dis*advantage. According to Judith Belk-Kanouse, Ph.D., poor listening during early development may result in problems with attention, memory, speech, language, reading, and other learning and communication skills. And poor listening in older children and teens manifests itself in issues in school, with friends, and with adults. Ultimately, it affects the quality of our relationships. What's worse, the habit of poor listening can be hard to break.

Being a good listener has a lot to do with attention span. If you have the capacity (and the patience) to sit quietly and focus on what the other person is saying, you're probably a good listener. Unfortunately, attention spans have become notoriously short. This is true for overwhelmed, overstressed, overstimulated adults—but it's even more of a problem for young people growing up in a world of endless distractions.

Yes, I am talking about technology. While it has brought with it numerous benefits, it has not done our listening skills any favors. As the tools of the Digital Age have pervaded every corner of our lives, we've been forced into multitasking almost as a lifestyle. And while multitasking may sharpen our brains in some ways, it's also a known culprit in shortening attention spans. And if you have no attention span, you have no listening skills.

If you have no attention span, you have no listening skills.

Absence in My Presence

In an article in the *New York Times* (April 17, 2011), "Keep Your Thumbs Still While I'm Talking to You," writer David Carr makes the case that the way we listen has changed. The significance is that those changes have become quite acceptable to some.

Carr points out that if you are having a conversation with someone and you look over the person's shoulder to see who may be more interesting in the room to talk with, you are being rude. However, if the person you are talking with has one eye on their smartphone and one eye on you through an entire conversation, that is considered "normal" and shows that he or she is a wired, well-connected person.

STOP!! A meaningful face-to-face conversation does not occur with another person while that person is texting someone else! And it's not crazy to think this way!

Anthony De Rosa, a product manager and programmer at Reuters, said in the same *New York Times* article that mobile connectedness has eroded fundamental human courtesies. "When people are out and they're among other people they need to just put everything down," he said while speaking at South by Southwest Interactive (SXSW), the popular annual conference for digital professionals.

> **A meaningful face-to-face conversation does not occur with another person while that person is texting someone else!**

These comments by De Rosa were met with loud applause. Ironic, considering the article shows pictures of an audience at SXSW "listening" to a speaker with their heads buried in laptops, iPads, and cell phones. The article even shows a woman in a hot tub with her attention focused on blogging on her iPad...while sharing the water with other people. In other words, De Rosa may have received a positive reaction to his comments, but did the audience actually hear him? It seems they were the worst offenders of all!

Maybe the lesson is that we want others to pay attention to us when *we're* talking, but it's okay to *not* listen when they are talking. (Personally, I question why someone would come to a live conference and not interact with those that he or she is face-to-face with. It seems to defeat the purpose.)

With adults behaving so inappropriately, it's hardly surprising that our kids are following suit. And it's not their fault. In many cases they're growing up with parents who multitask or spend much of their free time glued to the phone or computer (or both at the same time). Kids are used to having to make Mom and Dad tear their attention away from other things in order to ask a question or have a conversation. To them, it just seems like a "normal" way to live. And that's why many parents will need to change their own behavior as they seek to teach their children to engage well with others.

As you read on, remember: It's not that technology is bad. It's just that human interaction and face-to-face relationships are better.

It's not that technology is bad. It's just that human interaction and face-to-face relationships are better.

Good Listening Is an Instilled Value

Like many families, my household has a rule that all cell phones must be put away at dinnertime. This rule applies to all four members of our family. But honestly, a technology ban during meals *should* be the bare minimum. What we and other families need to do is to apply that dinnertime rule to *all* conversations in and out of the house. You just can't listen when you aren't paying attention.

Remember, children learn the most about how to communicate by communicating with us and by watching how we communicate with others. Parents today need to be good role models by taking the time to listen and to clearly send our own messages—and yes, I know it's not easy. But for a parent, this is as important as teaching good values to your children. Actually, it is exactly that.

You wouldn't allow your kids to engage in other rude behaviors, like talking back to adults or making fun of their friends. So why should dividing their attention during a conversation be any different? The truth is, such behavior is disrespectful and dismissive. Whether you're texting while talking or keeping an eye on the TV when you're supposed to be listening, you show the other person that she isn't important or interesting enough to keep you fully engaged. When you allow your kids (or yourself!) to get away with this behavior, you reinforce rudeness.

And it's not always about technology, either. As parents, most of us are guilty of "tuning out" our kids when we feel that something else is more pressing, or fobbing them off with vague, patronizing, or absentminded responses instead of really engaging with them. It's uncomfortable to admit, but those behaviors are just as bad as talking on the phone during dinner. Remember, kids are perceptive, and they can tell when you aren't fully "there" mentally. Our actions can easily say to them, "I don't really care what you have to say," which is, of course, hurtful to anyone.

Yes, I'm a parent, and I know that there are times when you simply *can't* give your kids all of your attention. After all, you need to take calls from your boss or give online bill-pay your full attention so that you don't accidentally mess up your checking account. At these time, it's best to be honest with your kids: "I know you're really excited to tell me about your field trip, and I really want to hear about it—but I need for you to be patient and wait until I'm finished so that I can really listen to you."

Bottom line? To teach kids to listen respectfully to us and to others, we need to listen respectfully *to them* in order to set the right example.

The Lost Art of Curious Listening

Despite almost universal and historic agreement on its importance, I think—considering the evidence mentioned earlier—we must conclude that listening is a lost art; perhaps more so than ever in this busy, hectic, and instant-everything world. We may hear what others are saying to us, but are we really listening?

In order to help your kids (and yourself) understand what the components of *good* listening are, I think it's helpful to first consider what keeps individuals from truly engaging with others. (After all, these pitfalls are things you'll want to avoid!) Depending on the ages of your children, you might want to talk to them about why each of the following listening characteristics isn't helpful. Or you could just keep your eyes open for teachable moments. For example, if your child comes home from school frustrated because her friend kept interrupting her story about your family's recent vacation, talk to your daughter about why it's both courteous and smart to let other people finish what they're telling you before chiming in.

Some noticeable characteristics of <u>bad</u> listeners are:

- Always interrupts
- Jumps to conclusions
- Finishes my sentences
- Changes the subject
- Is impatient
- Loses his/her temper
- Fidgets nervously
- Fails to maintain eye contact
- Climbs on a soapbox to demonstrate how much he/she knows about a subject
- Is doing something else while I'm talking

American author and editor Edgar Watson Howe pretty well summed up the essence of bad (or at least incomplete) listening when he wrote: "No man would listen to you talk if he didn't know it was his turn next."

What Does It Mean to Really Listen?

Like most skills, the art of listening well isn't just about avoiding pitfalls—it's also about doing specific things right. The fact is, good listening is *curious* listening, and it's an active process that is comprised of three basic steps:

1. **Hearing the Essence.** Hearing is pretty simple. It's the physical ability to pick up sounds with your ears and make sense of them—in other words, when you hear, you catch what the speaker is saying. To use a very simplistic example that your kids can relate to, a friend may say, "I'd love to see a movie with you!" If you can repeat the fact back to your pal, then you have heard what has been said.

2. **Getting It.** The next part of curiously listening happens when you take what you have heard and understand it in your own way instead of merely letting it go "in one ear and out the other," as the expression goes. In the example of the discussion with your friend, you might think, *Maybe she wants to go to a movie this weekend—I should check to see what's playing at the local theatres.*

3. **Confirmation.** Even if you're sure that you understand what the speaker has said, don't assume that you know what he or she *means.* Your friend may have wanted

to go to see a particular movie on opening night, she may not have a preference as long as the two of you get to go on an outing together, or she might just want to rent a DVD and watch it at home! So, we naturally ask questions to confirm assumptions like: "When do you want to get together?" "Is there a particular movie you'd like to see?" "Would you like to go to the theatre or stay home?" And we ask these questions until we have confirmed our assumptions.

In this example, curious listening may sound simple because if you want the facts, you need to ask fairly obvious questions in order to move forward. But are questions being asked in a majority of conversations? Are we really curious to know more facts? Curious listening is a powerful way to be a great listener and to show that you care enough to ask questions and follow up.

There's Something about the Way a Curious Listener Makes Us Feel

Curious listening is a structured hearing and questioning technique that helps you develop and enhance relationships through a stronger understanding of what is being conveyed both intellectually and emotionally. But in addition to the helpful and thoughtful questions a great listener asks, it's also what he or she *doesn't* say that is so powerful. Think about it: Have you ever been around someone who just wants to listen to you, who'd like to hear all about your day or your recent trip? Someone who is truly interested in *you*? Hmmm. I don't think you find people like that very often. But when you do, these individuals really stick out. That's because the act of listening shows that you care.

I work with an entrepreneur who runs a multimillion-dollar data architecture firm. He is so skilled at listening that our first meeting was almost uncomfortable. This man makes nearly unwavering eye contact, and his body language conveys his complete interest in everything that another person is saying. It certainly isn't typical. But since he started his firm when he was twenty years old, this man

The act of listening shows that you care.

has constantly been engaging in "investigative" work to find technical solutions for his clients. He does it by asking bold questions and listening intently to all the things the client has to say. And he says that often the client already has the solution if you focus on listening hard enough for it. (In other words, if a person knows her business inside and out, a solution is often right in front of her, albeit buried in her subconscious. Simply asking questions allows these potential solutions to "bubble up" to the surface so that the person can talk through them with you acting as a sounding board. Together, you can both come to conclusions about how to move forward.)

This entrepreneur's concentrated listening has served him well both personally and professionally. His unique ability to pay unwavering attention to the person he's with is the "X Factor" that allows him to connect with others on a different level, be memorable and likeable, and ultimately make almost twice the number of sales as most of his competitors in the United States.

Now, your kids might not grow up to be entrepreneurs, architects, or "business" people at all. But no matter what field they decide to pursue, I'm sure you can see why being a curious, attentive listener will benefit them as much as any technical skills they may acquire.

The More You Talk, the Less They Like You

Every summer, my family's neighborhood has an old-fashioned block party. We close off the streets and do our best to have a great time with lots of food, fun, and games for the kids. A few years ago, I was standing in the food line next to a neighbor named Amy. I hadn't seen her in months and barely knew her, but it was obvious she'd lost a lot of weight. I mentioned to Amy that I had noticed her svelte new figure and told her she looked great. Amy responded with a smile and told me that she had actually lost forty pounds. Wow! Obviously, I was intrigued. So I began to ask Amy more questions about how she lost the weight, what diet she used, what she was eating now, what her exercise regimen was, etc. I wanted to know everything because I was genuinely curious about how this neighbor had achieved her impressive success. For the next ten minutes, Amy answered all of my questions, and even told me about how her husband was responding to this weight loss!

Later that afternoon, another neighbor at the block party shared with me that she had just been talking with Amy, and that Amy was talking about how much she liked me. Me?? That was surprising; I hadn't said a word to Amy about myself. She didn't really know anything about me, my business, my kids, my house, my husband—nothing. I was simply curious, had asked Amy a lot of questions, and had listened to her interesting weight loss story—a topic that was very important to her. Later that night it hit me: Amy decided that she liked me because I listened to her, not because I talked. In fact, if I had steered the conversation toward myself, I assume that she would only have liked me…less!

The fact is, everybody likes to talk about themselves—not just the neighbor with whom I spoke while we were waiting for our hot dogs. That's why—even though it may seem the opposite of what is logical—we do not need to tell others how great we are or impress them with stories about ourselves and our accomplishments. It may be counter-intuitive, but the reality of human nature is that if you're genuinely curious and really listen to a person, he or she equates that personalized attention with caring—and often, that individual will quickly come to like you.

Good Listening Skills Bring Success in Business...and in Life!

Curiously listening is actually a unique skill these days, and it immediately sets the listener apart. Part of my job is to figure out what makes successful businesspeople successful, and I've discovered that no matter what product or service they're representing, these superstars are genuinely and transparently curious. And it is their likeability—sparked by their listening skills—that often closes the sale.

I'm not alone with my listening theory, either. In 1991, the United States Department of Labor Secretary's Commission on Achieving Necessary Skills (SCANS) identified five competencies and three foundation skills that are essential for those entering the workforce. Listening skills were among the foundation skills SCANS identified. Why? Well, in a nutshell, good listening skills make workers more productive, because the ability to listen carefully allows us to:

Curiously listening is actually a unique skill these days, and it immediately sets the listener apart.

- Better understand assignments and what is expected of us
- Build rapport with coworkers, bosses, and clients
- Show support

- Work better in a team-based environment
- Resolve problems with customers, coworkers, and bosses
- Answer questions
- Find underlying meanings in what others say

In other words—listening is the first step in truly connecting with others. And as any parent will notice, the skills listed above aren't just useful in the workplace. They're also good to have in the classroom, on the soccer field, in ballet class, and at the neighborhood pool party.

Can Listening Save You from Getting Sued?

How important is listening? In his best-selling book *Blink*, Malcolm Gladwell tells the amazing story of a study conducted by a medical researcher to determine the likelihood of doctors being sued by their patients. According to Gladwell, "Roughly half of the doctors had never been sued. The other half had been sued at least twice." The research disclosed specific differences between the two groups. "The surgeons who had never been sued," Gladwell reported, "spent more than three minutes longer with each patient than those who had been sued did."

What took place during those extra three minutes some of the doctors spent with their patients? They allowed time for questions and encouraged their patients to talk. They paid attention, and they listened. They showed that they cared.

If a patient's procedure went awry, of course, a lawsuit *was* filed. But in the case of these "listening surgeons," someone else received that dreaded stack of papers. In documented cases, it was usually the internist or radiologist against whom the patient brought a lawsuit. Why? Because these patients actually liked the *surgeon*, and we don't sue people we like!

Now, poor listening skills might not send you and your kids into litigation, but the point is that it can have very negative consequences. Why risk those consequences when listening just a little more closely will improve conversations and relationships for all involved?

An Acquired Skill

Although listening is a skill that can be learned, very little has ever been done about teaching it. As children, we began "tuning out" our parents; and as we grew, we applied that same technique to our teachers and other adults. So, it's little wonder that by the time we began to make our way in the world, we didn't listen to our boss, our coworkers, our customers, or our prospects—or they to us! Not only weren't we taught *how* to listen, we were never taught the *importance* of listening.

Now, I'll be honest with you—there's probably nothing you can do to prevent your kids from tuning you out, at all, ever. (They're kids; that's what they do!) But you *can* take steps to make sure that they aren't in tune-out mode 24/7. Listening well—in other words, listening curiously—is an acquired skill that parents can develop in their children. Here are some starting points:

> Not only weren't we taught *how* to listen, we were never taught the *importance* of listening.

Curious Listening for Kids

- **Practice active listening with them.** We've all had conversations during which we wondered if the other person was even on the same plane of reality, and they're not fun—no one wants to feel as though they're talking to a brick wall. To be a good listener, you must *act like a good listener*. That's harder than it sounds, because in our instant-access, wired world, most of us have worked our entire lives to effectively tune out all of the information that relentlessly bombards us 24/7. The good news is that just by changing our physical body language we can look like someone who wants to receive information (instead of someone who's trying to block it out). In essence, our faces say it all. Here are three things to work on with your kids (as well as explanations as to why they are effective):

First, tell your kids to make eye contact. Your eyes pick up the nonverbal signals that all people send out when they are speaking. Plus, when you look at the speaker, you will complete the eye contact that she is trying to make. The truth is, a speaker will work harder at sending out information when she sees a receptive listener.

Secondly, coach your children to make use of facial expressions. If you are paying attention to what someone else is saying, your face will move and display the range of emotions that indicate that you are following what the speaker is saying. By moving your face with the conversation, you can better concentrate on what the person is saying, thus actively capturing information.

Lastly, teach your kids to acknowledge what's been said. Acknowledgment can be something as basic as a nod of the head or a simple "uh huh." You aren't necessarily agreeing with the person; you are merely indicating that you are listening. Using body language and other signs to demonstrate you are listening also reminds you to pay attention, and not to let your mind wander. Asking an occasional question or making a comment is helpful too, because these things indicate that you're interested and demonstrate that you understand what's being said. (Just don't interrupt!)

You can easily practice doing these things during all of the conversations you and your children have with one another.

- **Discourage interrupting.** Regardless of age, we've *all* been guilty of interrupting another person from time to time. Whether we're correcting another's error or adding a piece of information we think is vital, it can be difficult to wait our turn…and even more so for kids whose attention spans and supply of patience are shorter. Whenever you catch your kids cutting into a conversation, gently remind them to let the other person finish before they begin to talk. Explain to them that speakers appreciate having the chance to say everything they would like to say without being interrupted. Plus, when you interrupt with your comments, the other person might feel like you aren't listening, even if you really are. And you can't truly listen if you're busy thinking about what you want to say next!

- **Outlaw DWD (discussing while distracted).** Emphasize to your kids: "If your attention is divided, you aren't being a good listener." Whether the culprit is a computer, a smartphone, a television, or even what's going on outside the window, always redirect your kids' attention when you see it wandering. If they're having trouble focusing, tell them to change their body position and concentrate on the speaker's words. Ultimately, when your kids learn to focus solely on the conversation that is happening when they're at home, they'll carry that habit to school, to practice, to outings with friends, and more.

- **Teach them to look for the real meaning.** There's often a difference between what people say and what they mean. (Case in point: How many times have you responded with a perky "Fine!" when others ask you how you're doing— even though you may be one email away from a total breakdown?) It's important to explain to your kids that they can't always take the things they hear at face value— sometimes they'll need to read between the lines and try to understand what's *really* driving people. A good way to gauge how someone you're talking to is *really* feeling is to pay attention to nonverbal cues and/or to consider what emotions they might be feeling.

  Talk to your children about paying attention to facial expressions, body language, tone of voice, etc. Kids already respond to these things on a subconscious level (after all, most youngsters shape right up when Mom or Dad gives them "the look"), but they may need you to help them make a conscious connection between, say, the fact that someone's crossed arms mean that he is upset or uncomfortable. Here are three ways to do that:

  1. You can use family TV time or movie night to help your kids practice identifying another person's true mood or feelings simply by asking, for example, "That character just said he's happy to hear that his friend was elected student body

president, but do you think he's *really* feeling that way? Why not?"

2. Another great way to help your kids develop an accurate grasp of nonverbal cues is to play a game of charades. They'll be forced to actively think about what types of expressions, poses, etc. convey certain emotions.

3. And, of course, you can use real-life situations as teaching aids! For example, your teenager's friend may say she isn't upset that your daughter can't make it to her birthday party because of a previous engagement, but her facial expression or body language might give away her true feelings. Teach your kids to pay attention to these details and to know how to react. In the above example, the teen might say, "I really wish I could come to your party. I know it won't be exactly the same, but can we hang out next Friday night? I am sure my mom would be willing to take us to the movies!"

- **Help them tap into the power of questions.** I've said before that asking questions can be a good way to let another person know that you are listening to what he has to say. Help your children take questions to the next level by using them to stimulate conversations and to make discussions more engaging. A fun way to develop this skill is to practice the "interview technique." (Note: This method is especially helpful for kids who are shy and who may initially be uncomfortable offering information and observations of their own during conversation.)

Ask your child to pretend that she is a reporter writing a story about the person with whom she's speaking. Her job is to find out as many interesting things as possible, and to do that, she needs to ask questions to get the conversation flowing. Let's say your child's friend recently went to the beach. Your child's side of the conversation might go, "Where did you stay? Oh, so your family stayed at a house instead of a hotel so you could take your dog. What kind of dog do you have? Do you always take it on vacation with you? If you had to name your best vacation ever, what would it be….and why?" etc. Point out to your child that by asking questions, she took one sentence from her friend—"I went to the beach"—and turned it into a full-fledged, meaningful conversation!

You and your child might also get into the habit of "interviewing" each other about your days, your favorite restaurants, your best friends, your favorite movies, and more. It's a good way to show your child how curious listening can lead the conversation in all kinds of unexpected directions as your questions spark other thoughts and associations in the person. Point out the fact that your curiosity can help you learn a lot about the other person that you didn't know before, and that he or she will almost always end up liking you more because of the genuine interest you have shown.

- **Instruct them not to force conversations.** Of course, the interview technique isn't always appropriate or welcome! Sometimes people just don't feel like talking in general; other times they might want to avoid a specific topic. Explain this to your children, and help them to understand that if someone isn't open and forthcoming, it might be time to pack away the "curious" part of "curious listening." (In these types of situations, the ability to accurately interpret nonverbal cues and tone of voice will be very useful!)

  For example, you might gently suggest that your daughter stop asking her older brother why he didn't make the varsity basketball team this year (after all, he was a useful member of the junior varsity team last year!). Help her to realize that forcing her brother to dwell on this topic makes him feel very bad about himself, and that figuring out the "why" won't change what's already happened.

- **Give them "key words" for listening.** In order to be a good listener, other people have to first be willing to talk to you. Especially in touchy or unpleasant situations, individuals often need an invitation to share. Teach your kids to say, "If you need a friend, I'm around," "Would you like to talk about what happened?" or, "Don't worry, this conversation will stay between you and me."

- **Teach them to look for the remarkable.** "Find the remarkable in conversations with others," says Sunny Bates, an entrepreneur who maintains a network of some of the most prominent people in the world. "There is *always* something that a person says in every conversation that is truly remarkable." Bates sits on the boards of many organizations and foundations and is also on the advisory board for the TED Conference that gathers the world's leading thinkers and doers together each year. She says that it doesn't matter if the person is prominent, famous, or just an everyday Joe or Jane. The key is to listen for and remember the remarkable if you want to make a genuine and lasting connection.

Listening for the remarkable isn't a skill that's limited to businesspeople or even to adults. Teach your children to find and remember the most interesting and noteworthy things in the conversations they have. You can help them practice. Tell them that main points are often conveyed at the beginning or end of a conversation, or may be repeated several times.

For example, after visiting Grandma, ask your daughter what she remembers from the conversation. Perhaps Grandma hasn't been feeling well and is suffering from back pain. The next time you visit, ask your daughter on your way over if she remembers what was wrong with Grandma last time you saw her. Suggest that she check in with Grandma today. It's as simple as asking, "How is your back feeling today, Grandma?"

Listening for the remarkable will strengthen your kid's listening skills as well as the quality of their relationships! In fact, their relationships might become more "remarkable"!

Seven Simple Yet Powerful Listening Tips

I've already covered the following listening tips in the previous section, but you may still find this "cheat sheet" useful. Consider showing it to your tween or teen (or even spouse!).

1. **Give Your Full Attention:** Give your full attention on the person who is speaking. Don't look at your computer, BlackBerry, or gaze somewhere else.

2. **Focus:** Make sure your mind is focused on the person in front of you—if only for a short period of time. If you feel your mind wandering, change the position of your body and try to concentrate on the speaker's words.

3. **Don't Interrupt:** Let the other person finish before you begin to talk. Speakers appreciate having the chance to say everything they would like to say without being interrupted. When you interrupt with your comments it feels to the other person like you aren't listening, even if you really are. And you can't truly listen if you're busy thinking about what you want to say next.

4. **Pay Special Attention for the Key Points:** The main ideas are the most important points a person wants to get across. They may be mentioned at the start or end or they may be repeated a number of times.

5. **Watch for Nonverbal Cues**: A good listener knows that being attentive to what the speaker *doesn't* say is as important as being attentive to what he/she does say. Look for nonverbal cues such as facial expressions and posture to get the full gist of what the speaker is telling you.

6. **Ask Questions:** Ask questions to clarify what the person who is talking is saying. Repeat what they have said in your own words so you can be sure your understanding is correct.

7. **Respond:** Sit up straight, look directly at the person talking, and occasionally lean in to the conversation. Nod to show with your body that you are listening. Also give verbal acknowledgments ("yes," or, "hmmm," or, "I see") to show that you hear what they are saying.

Here's an interesting fact: The six letters that make up the word "listen" can be rearranged to make up another word that's essential if we're to be good listeners—"silent." By your silence, you're conveying to the speaker this message: "You matter to me." So ultimately, to strengthen their connections, the most effective building block your children can use is their ability to listen—quietly and carefully. As the late Dean Rusk—U.S. Secretary of State under Presidents John F. Kennedy and Lyndon B. Johnson—noted: "One of the best ways to persuade others is with your ears—by listening to them."

We're probably all familiar with the old adage that the reason God gave us two ears but only one mouth is so that we'd do twice as much listening as talking. Yet, we've somehow come to believe that talking is the way to impress others so they'll recognize how smart we are, how much we know, and what we can do for them.

Listening is not an easy skill to learn; it takes discipline and concentration. But it's still a critical human value to impart to children—for their sakes and for the benefit of those around them.

3

Leadership through Effective Communication

If you want your child to stand out, having good grades and being well-mannered sure helps. But if you really want him or her to stand out, teach your child to have a conversation with an adult. When your child is able to do this comfortably, it's a sign of great things to come.

When you're a kid, having a meaningful conversation with an adult takes confidence. It requires you to step outside of your comfort zone because you're presenting your thoughts and opinions to someone who is more powerful than you. Those ideas must also be logical, organized, and well thought-out, because since kids don't have the personal authority to enforce their ideas, they will need to succeed on their own merits. In other words, talking to an adult also requires you to step outside of "kid mode" and connect on a

Teach your child to have a conversation with an adult.

more complex and sophisticated level. Finally, when you're a kid who is connecting with adults, you must be able to put someone else's needs and preferences above your own by considering what a grown-up would want to talk about.

When you think about it, many of the skills that a child must employ to interact confidently with grown-ups are also the traits of good leaders. Because adults *are* authority figures—at least to kids—teaching your children to interact confidently with them is a way to encourage the development of leadership skills naturally and organically. Kids can "lead" adults only through effective communication.

I'm starting out this chapter by asking you to, as often as possible, put your kids in situations where they carry on conversations with adults. It may be the single most important thing you do in your quest to raise engaging children. (And when you get to Chapter 7 you'll see that I've provided plenty of scenarios occurring in everyday life that your child can take advantage of to practice this skill.)

Of course, the ability to converse with adults is only one piece of the picture. In the pages to come I will describe some of the other skills that enable your children to develop and hone their "leadershipability."

Many, many times throughout my career, I've noticed that despite their different personalities and responsibilities, great leaders in business (and in life!) have in common a series of skills that allow them to succeed in managing, influencing, and persuading others. And here's the great news: When it comes to learning these skills, kids are in the best possible position. They can be taught and guided to become leaders without the pressures that exist later in life.

This chapter will offer some suggestions for how parents can instill

> **Kids can be taught and guided to become leaders without the pressures that exist later in life.**

and encourage these valuable traits in their children. But first, let's discuss the nature of leadership in a bit more depth.

Does Social Intelligence Translate into Leadership Success?

It's no secret that when the theories of social intelligence (as discussed in Chapter 1) are applied in a person's life, he or she will enjoy better personal relationships as well as significantly more business success. (In fact, it's been empirically proven.) But the benefits of being socially intelligent can go much farther than that. The fact is, people who have higher levels of social intelligence and engagement abilities are also the great leaders. And great leaders can do one very significant thing: They get people to act. The "how" behind it might surprise you.

In 1998, Daniel Goleman published an article entitled "What Makes a Leader?" in the *Harvard Business Review*. Soon afterward, people started to buzz about Goleman's thoughts on the role that bonding and relationships play in effective business and leadership. More specifically, they were interested in Goleman's assertion that when leaders exhibit empathy and become attuned to others' moods, they literally affect both their own and their teams' brain chemistry. People began to understand that if you want to become a better leader, it's helpful to learn the kinds of social behavior that reinforce the brain's social circuitry.

However, it's important to realize that it's not enough to simply *act* in a certain way. In order to tap into the true power of social intelligence, you've got to *be* a certain way. As Goleman puts it, "Leading effectively is, in other words, less about mastering situations—or even social skill sets—than about developing a genuine interest in and talent for fostering positive feelings in the people whose cooperation and support you need."

The idea that leaders need social skills is not a new one, of course. In 1920, Columbia University psychologist Edward L. Thorndike pointed out that "the best mechanic in a factory may fail as a foreman for lack of social intelligence." Harvard's Claudio Fernández-Aráoz also found in an analysis of new C-level executives that those who had been hired for their self-discipline, drive, and intellect were sometimes later fired for lacking basic social skills. In other words, the people Fernández-Aráoz studied were incredibly intelligent, but their inability to get along socially on the job was detrimental to their success.

What Causes People to Act, Buy, and Follow?

Before moving on, I'd like to offer a bit more detailed explanation as to why genuinely caring about others influences their own thoughts and behaviors. It has to do with behavioral neuroscience and *mirror neurons*, which are located in widely dispersed areas of the brain. Italian neuroscientists discovered mirror neurons by accident while monitoring a particular cell in a monkey's brain that fired only when the monkey raised its arm. One day, a lab assistant lifted an ice cream cone to his own mouth and triggered a reaction in the monkey's cell. It was the first evidence that the brain is peppered with neurons that mimic, or mirror, what another being does.

This previously unknown class of brain cells operates as neural Wi-Fi, allowing us to navigate our social world. When we consciously or unconsciously detect someone else's emotions through their actions, our mirror neurons reproduce those emotions. Collectively, these neurons create an instant sense of shared experience, and that causes a feeling that precedes one's actions.[iii] In other words, we truly can cause a feeling in others through our actions. So, what is it about being socially intelligent that gets people to act, buy, and follow? It is quite simple. It's how you make them feel.

> We truly can cause a feeling in others through our actions.

iii   Boyatzis, Richard, and Daniel Goleman. "Social Intelligence and the Biology of Leadership." *Harvard Business Review*, September 2008, 74-81.

Because of the way social intelligence works, when we attempt to teach our kids values, empathy, kindness, and more, we're not only doing the right thing—we're helping to shape their ability to connect and, thus, their future success.

Are Leaders Born or Created?

With all of that said, let's look at social intelligence—and how it relates to leadership—in parenting terms. This is where we as parents must realize that the way our children think about and relate to others starts *now*, when they're young. Yes, we are all born with some leadership skills, and as is the case with any strength, some of us are more strongly gifted than others. However, I truly believe that the greatest leaders are created and cultivated throughout their lives, not just "born that way." In other words, no matter what leadership skills or traits a child is born with, she will not be as effective as possible if she is not able to make others feel emotions that motivate and drive them, nor will she make much progress if she is unable to think and plan clearly herself.

I have identified four traits that good leaders share. (There are others as well, but these are a few of the most notable.) The sections below explain how you can help nurture them in your children:

Leadership Trait One: Empathy

In order to effectively lead, you need to have a good understanding of how your words, actions, and decisions affect others…which means you need to have a strongly developed sense of empathy. We covered this topic in detail in Chapter 1, so here's a short refresher course.

Teaching your children empathy (more specifically, breaking them out of their "me, me, me" mindsets) is certainly easier said than done. However, repeatedly drawing attention back to the way others feel makes this possible and effective. In addition to following the suggestions from Chapter 1, here are some questions you can ask your child to sharpen his sense of empathy, thus developing in him one of the key traits of a good leader.

- Do you know how others feel?
- How can you tell how others feel? (If your child needs a hint, remind her of your discussion regarding body language, facial expressions, tone of voice, etc.)
- What does it mean to put yourself in someone else's shoes?
- What can you do to help someone who is feeling a certain way?
- Think of a time when you hurt someone's feelings—how did it happen? How did you feel about the situation? What could you have done to make the situation better?

- How would your school be better if more students and teachers changed the way they showed that they care about others? Do you think it would be a big change or a small change?

Please, I urge you to revisit the empathy tips in Chapter 1. I cannot emphasize enough how important it is to nurture your child's ability to understand the feelings of those around him. It is the heart and soul of being able to engage and connect with—and yes, lead—other people.

Leadership Trait Two: Organization

Leaders are generally expected to have good organization skills. It's not hard to see why. If you can't find your presentation notes or forget to bring a copy of your team's proposal to a client meeting, you might never be promoted beyond entry level—never mind be given a position of authority! And beyond personal accountability, the ability to build structure is a key factor in leading others through projects because structure fosters a clear vision going forward.

But that's just the beginning of what being organized means. It's more than having a place for everything and making sure your surroundings are neat and orderly. Rather, it's a way of approaching whatever comes your way with logic and good sense. It means you're able to look at a complex set of circumstances and say, "If I do this, then I'll be able to do *this*, which will set me up to do that…" and so forth. It means you actively anticipate problems and take steps to prevent them.

People who are organized don't usually run around like the proverbial chicken with its head cut off; they make progress and get things done on or before schedule. Their approach to life gives them an edge that allows them to do things just a little

People who are organized don't usually run around like the proverbial chicken with its head cut off.

better and more efficiently than their peers…which is why organized people often become leaders.

Here's just one example of how organization can impact your professional life: An important meeting is scheduled for this morning, so after leaving home you drive straight to work. There's no need to stop for gas (possibly making you late), because you filled up your tank last night. Once you're in the office (a few minutes early, as it happens), you don't have to rush around looking for your presentation notes, because you gathered them up and paper clipped them together yesterday. Before the meeting starts, you have time to converse for a few minutes with the VIPs who are also there. And *that* means, when they need someone with your skill set in the future, you're the person they'll think of.

Ultimately, people who are in "the right place at the right time" are usually there because of a series of prudent decisions leading up to that moment. Those decisions didn't just start in the twenty-four hours preceding the moment, either. No, this type of organization—the type that fosters good leadership—is often the result of creating the right habits from childhood on.

That said, here are several ways to cultivate the skill of organization in your children:

- **Create a to-do checklist (or two, or more!).** Whether it's a list of chores or homework assignments for school, your child can cross off tasks as they are completed, thus gaining both a sense of accomplishment and the foundation for organizational skills. If he's old enough, make sure he's the one making and updating the lists, too.

- **Make a calendar.** From school field trips to sports practices to music lessons, playdates, and more, chances are your child is busy. Instead of being her social coordinator, ask her to write down her own appointments. Look at the calendar together each morning so that you *both* know what's coming up!

- **Think ahead.** Now that your child is in charge of his own calendar, help him to consider how to prepare for upcoming events. For example, if there's a baseball game tomorrow, he might want to pack his sports bag tonight. This will save a lot of last-minute scrambling and stress!

- **Enforce accountability.** If your child falls through on a commitment because of a lack of organization, don't berate—but *do* point out that things might have been different if he had been better prepared. Ask him to help you do a "post-mortem" to figure out the first place he veered off track and how it led to subsequent missteps. Then talk about how he can prevent his mistake from happening again. On the flip side, if your child succeeds because of *good* organization, praise him!

- **Plan some projects.** In addition to daily habits, structured projects can also be very valuable in developing organizational skills. Here are three to consider:

    1. **Banish bedroom mess.** Unless you have a *very* unusually organized child, chances are her room could use a little tidying. Ask her to gather up all loose items, as well as things that tend to become jumbled in a pile. Then help her to sort them into categories—for example, toys, books, school supplies, accessories, etc. You might consider placing them in labeled boxes or clear Tupperware containers. Once everything is more orderly, help your child to set up a system for putting her clothes, toys, books, etc. in their places all of the time—and point out that life runs a lot more smoothly when you know where everything is!

    2. **Cook a meal.** Ask your child to plan and cook a meal (perhaps with your help, depending on

age) for your family. He'll have to utilize many organizational skills, such as pre-planning, gathering ingredients, precision, and time management.

3. **Celebrate a birthday.** You don't want to make your child do all the work for her birthday party, but you *can* get her involved in the planning. She can help with the guest list, sending out invitations, and sorting through RSVPs. She can also help you decide what you'll need to buy and prepare, such as paper plates, party favors, and food.

Leadership Trait Three: Problem Solving

One of the key traits of a leader is his or her ability to solve problems and make good decisions. Seth Godin, a world-renowned author, entrepreneur, and speaker, has shared his thoughts on the value of problem solving and how critical it is that our children learn this skill. Godin feels that problem solving is not taught properly in schools, even though it is one of the

One of the key traits of a leader is his or her ability to solve problems and make good decisions.

most crucial skills to master for success in many areas of life, including business.

Godin makes a strong case by pointing out that schools are organized around obedience—they are organized around taking tests and training students to follow instructions, which leads to obedience and self-control. No, those aren't *bad* qualities in and of themselves. However, leaders in business and in life aren't necessarily compliant; they stand outside of conventional thinking because of their excellent problem-solving skills.

"We organize our companies around obedience as well," Godin said in a blog post on September 13, 2011. "From the résumé we use to hire to the training programs to the annual budgets, revenue targets, and reviews we create, the model employee is someone who does what he's told. Compliant sergeants rarely become great generals."[iv]

The point is, helping children develop good problem-solving skills can help them develop as leaders. Being able to approach a predicament or setback with confidence, knowing that it can be resolved, will boost your child's confidence and greatly empower him. He'll also be honing his commonsense skills at the same time. As a parent, one of the best ways to develop this skill in your children is to help them work through their own problems. Here's how you can help:

iv   Godin, Seth. "Confusing obedience with self-control." *Seth Godin's Blog.*
     13 September 2011. <http://sethgodin.typepad.com/seths_blog/2011/09/
     confusing-obedience-with-self-contro.html> (1 October 2011).

- **Identify the problem.** Whether it's a fight with a sibling, a disagreement with a friend, or an issue at school, make sure that your child knows that step one is correctly identifying what the issue is. Explain that when things aren't going well, our emotions can bubble up strongly and cloud our ability to accurately understand what's going on. Tell your child, for example, that while she may *feel* that her teacher is picking on her, the difficulty might actually be stemming from the fact that her homework assignments have been turned in late a few times in the past month. Always encourage your child to think about things from the other person's perspective!

- **Identify the goal.** Obviously, your child wants to resolve whatever issue he's facing...but what does that resolution actually look like? Ask him to describe his goal: maybe to stop fighting with his friend, or to figure out how to better study for his next test.

- **Figure out solutions.** Talk about how your child might be able to achieve her goal, and try to think of several solutions. Then, discuss the pros and cons of each. Ask questions like, "So, what do you think would happen if you acted this way?"

    For example, let's return to the example of your child having problems with her teacher because several homework assignments have been handed in late recently. One "solution" would be for your daughter to simply endure the friction until the end of the school year—but it wouldn't be a very prudent one. A big improvement on this plan would be for her to make an extra effort to meet all of her deadlines from now on. And the best solution of all would be for your daughter to talk to her teacher in order to first apologize, and then devise a plan to get back on track. Perhaps it would require cutting back on an afterschool activity that's taking too much time, or engaging a tutor to strengthen her understanding of the subject.

After discussing each of these three options with your daughter, point out that number three will accomplish the most because it enables her to engage directly with the source of the problem: her teacher. If possible, it's always best to try to repair relationships—not just circumstances.

- **Identify the best option.** Now, it's time for your child to put his plan into action! Be there for support and encouragement, but don't fix things yourself.

Be there for support and encouragement, but don't fix things yourself.

Of course, not all "problems" that need to be solved start with a fractious relationship or a mistake. Sometimes they aren't sparked by anything going wrong at all—you simply need to figure out a way to get from point A to point B. For example, maybe your child wants to be able to buy some souvenirs on your upcoming vacation, but he currently has only $10 to his name. How might he earn more?

Or perhaps your daughter wants to try for a speaking role in the school play, although she has no prior acting experience. What can she do to improve her chances of being cast?

Whenever your child isn't sure how to get from where he is to where he wants to be, encourage him to think through the steps listed above. His independence, confidence, and effectiveness will grow each time progress is made. And instead of relying on others to help him move forward (in other words, being a follower), he'll develop into a true leader.

Leadership Trait Four: Goal Setting

Setting goals is another activity that will help develop leadership skills in children. After all, it's important to be able to set realistic goals and then reach them if you want to be able to positively influence and guide others (and advance in a good direction yourself!).

Believe it or not, many would-be leaders stall when it comes to goal setting. Oh, they've got the people skills necessary to head a team. They can deal with any issues that might crop up, and they're rarely slowed down by disorganization. But moving forward prudently and effectively? Well, that can be a problem. You see, a good leader must be able to know when to move and how far to move—or not. Aim too high, too soon, and your organization might fall on its face. Proceed too cautiously, and it will be outstripped by the competition.

Time and time again, I have noticed that a leader's ability to set goals can mean the difference between success and failure.

If you're skeptical of just how instrumental smart goal setting can be, think of your dream vacation. You can wish all your life to spend a few weeks in a tropical paradise or exploring the country from which your ancestors hailed, but unless you make plans to achieve this desire, you'll be stuck looking at pictures in brochures. (And on the other hand, if you hop on a plane without much prior thought, you could find yourself in a mountain of debt when you get home.) To reach that far-off destination, you've got to keep the end goal—the vacation itself—in mind, while making and achieving smaller supporting goals, like saving money, planning to take time off work, and detailing your itinerary. It's a simplistic example, but you can see that a failure to proactively set appropriate goals can prevent you from getting what you want. And in business, you can lose much more than a chance to relax and enjoy yourself away from home—you could lose opportunities, clients, money, respect, and position.

Clearly, it's important for a leader to be able to work toward his organization's vision by moving from achievable, measurable milestone to achievable, measurable milestone, all while keeping the bigger picture in mind. If you accustom your child to doing these things while he's young, he won't be overwhelmed by the need to plan for his own future— and possibly those of others—when he is an adult. Plus, your child's confidence will grow when goals are consistently reached. Here are some ways to help your children set healthy goals and then achieve them:

- **Discuss the difference between long- and short-term goals.** It's important to identify right off the bat whether a goal is something that can be accomplished by next Friday (like completing a Lego kit) or something that's going to take significantly longer (like applying to college). Knowing the scope will have a big impact on your achievement strategy!

- **Break it down.** For all but the smallest goals, it's helpful to break down what needs to be done into smaller steps. Your child will find goal achievement more manageable and will be much less overwhelmed. (Plus, she'll feel a lot more gratification and sense of accomplishment on the way!)

- **Get on a schedule.** Help your child decide when his ultimate deadline is (if it isn't set in stone already), as well as when he wants to complete his various "stepping-stone" goals. He might find it helpful to write these dates down in a planner or on a calendar—this will help him feel more organized and in control. (Plus, what gets scheduled gets done. The reverse isn't always true.)

- **Give them some motivation.** As an adult, you've had a good bit of practice with self-motivation, so you don't necessarily need someone encouraging you every step of the way. You also have the power to reward yourself with a trip to the spa, a new book, or a night out with the guys when you achieve something great. Remember that your kids don't have the same abilities yet. Encourage and praise them as they make progress, and also consider deciding beforehand on a reward that your child can enjoy when she succeeds. (This could be anything from going out for ice cream to getting a new bike.)

- **Help them see how they've grown.** After a goal has been achieved, talk to your child about how he has grown. Help him to identify any skills he may have acquired and discuss how they can be used in the future.

The Lowdown on Raising Leaders (Abbreviated Version!)

I could write an entire book on what parents can do to encourage the development of leadership traits in their children. Since I don't have that much space, here are a few more brief tips on how you can cultivate a future leader:

- **Give your child a choice.** As early as preschool, we start hearing about what our kids' résumés "need" to look like if we want them to get into a good college, get a good job, etc. However, don't allow others' ideas to decide what your child's life looks like. Let him have some input when it comes to choosing extracurricular activities (like which sport to play or musical instrument to choose) instead of dictating what's going to happen. Having agency from a young age will build confidence and help diminish indecisiveness. (Plus, pursuing activities he's passionate about will help your child's success much more than fitting himself into a formula will.)

- **Let your child teach.** If there are younger siblings (or cousins or neighbors), ask your child to teach her less-experienced peer. The "subject" could be how to color by numbers, how to ride a bike, how to water flowers, and much more!

- **Ask for your child's input.** When a family decision needs to be made, ask for your child's opinion. (For example, "Should Dad take the new job he's been offered? It would be a promotion for him, but our family would have to move to another city." Or, "What restaurant would you like us to eat at tonight?") Even if you don't take your child's advice, he'll know that he is valued and respected—and he'll also become comfortable with discussing more serious matters from an early age.

- **Let your children fight their own battles.** Sometimes we have to step in as parents because our children can't reasonably be expected to navigate the adult world alone. After all, it's our *job* to protect our kids! But when we do everything for them, we don't ultimately do them any favors. Whenever appropriate, ask your child to take the lead. For example, she is capable of asking her teacher for extra help. She can call her friend to say, "I'm sorry—something came up and I won't be able to attend your birthday party," etc.

- **Teach your children to be positive thinkers.** If your child grows up as a pessimist, he'll always operate from a place of fear and negativity—which is not conducive to good leadership! In order to do great things, your child must first believe that it's possible for him to accomplish them. (The following sidebar, "Infuse Your Vocabulary with Leadership Words," will help you to infuse positive thoughts and words into your child's life.)

- **Encourage creativity.** Effective leaders think outside the box and are not limited by "the way things have always been done." From art projects to puzzles to researching an interesting topic on the Internet, fill your child's life with things that stretch her imagination and expose her to new ways of thinking and doing.

- **Give your child good role models.** Early on, expose your children to people whose lives are full of accomplishment, creativity, and fulfillment. You can read biographies of admired figures, go see a guest speaker at a local college, or talk to a family friend your child admires. Knowing these people—and their stories—will give your child something healthy to aspire to. Also, be sure to point out that a leader doesn't have to have a title like "VP, CEO, or owner." There are many ways to lead, including through writing, mentoring, influencing others positively, teaching, etc.

- **Instill strong morals in your children.** Make sure your children have a sense of fairness, humility, accountability, perspective, integrity, etc. This will earn them respect throughout their lives and will ensure that their own success does not come at the expense of others.

Yes, I know—all of this is easier said than done. It takes time, effort, patience, and persistence to help your child become a confident and effective leader. For instance, I'm very proud of my fifteen-year-old son, Shane. Like all children (and in fact, all humans!), he's a work in progress. Every year, he exhibits more and more great leadership skills. He enjoys setting goals, making to-do lists, and thinking about and solving problems. He also leads students in school because he's not afraid to speak up and take a position if he feels strongly about something (although sometimes it is not appreciated by the teachers!).

As Shane's mother, I can see numerous areas of his life to which he has applied the leadership skills he has developed. (He'd probably tell you that they have been most useful in his pursuit of hockey, his favorite thing in the world.) As for me, I'd say that right now Shane is mostly a good leader of himself, not necessarily others. And that's okay! His father and I know that Shane must be able to govern himself well before he is able to influence others. We are grateful for all of the skills he has developed, and we know—and always keep in mind— that he needs to continue to work on his communication skills to reach the next level: translating his personal skills to leading others. (See Chapter 7 of this book for exercises you can do with your children regardless of which area they need to improve.)

Infuse Your Vocabulary with Leadership Words

Especially if your child tends to be pessimistic or uncertain of himself, I have found that teaching him what I call "leadership words" can really help him to take charge of himself and others.

Think about it: If a child gets into the habit of using powerful, engaging words instead of weak ones (even if she *is* feeling hesitant or negative), her thoughts and thus her actions will be retrained in that direction. Because perception is reality, in a very real way, her words will promote self-esteem in herself and in others.

On a very simple level, here are some examples of what leadership words look like:

- **Instead of saying, "I might," say, "I will."**
- **Instead of saying, "I hope," say, "I know."**
- **Instead of saying, "This is a big problem," say, "This is a complicated situation."**
- **Instead of saying, "I made a stupid mistake," say, "I learned something important today."**
- **And, of course, *always* avoid saying, "I can't!" because the phrase becomes a self-fulfilling prophecy. A good alternative might be: "This**

looks like a big challenge, and it's going to take a lot of hard work. But I know I can do it!"

Now I'd like to show you how you can infuse leadership words into everyday situations. The first has happened in my house many times (and I suspect in yours also), and the second is also likely to crop up in your child's future:

- Your child has a big math test coming up tomorrow. He has been studying all week, but since numbers aren't his strong point, he's nervous despite his preparation. As he clears his books off the kitchen table, he mutters, "I hope I'll pass the test tomorrow. Pre-algebra is a problem for me, and I'm afraid I'm gonna bomb the class."

  First remind your child that he has done his best to prepare, and that his hours of studying have done a lot of good. Then suggest that he say, "I know I'll be ready for the test. After I get a good night's sleep, I'll look over my notes one more time in the morning. Pre-algebra is a challenge, but I know I'm smart enough to meet it."

- It's finally time to apply to college, and your teen has realized exactly what that process entails: school visits, creating a résumé, getting teacher recommendations, writing essays, scheduling interviews and standardized tests, and more (on top of her regular homework and activities!). After starting her fourth online application, she bursts out, "I'm never going to finish this process! I'm so overwhelmed—these applications are like taking an extra class in school that I'm not even getting credit for. And even if I do manage to complete all of this work, there's no guarantee that any of these colleges will accept me. I wish I could just give up."

First, acknowledge that your child has a point—then help her to realize that her college glass is much fuller than she's making it out to be. Suggest that she say to herself, "Going to college is going to be one of the biggest milestones in my life, so it makes sense that I'm going to have to put a lot of preparation and work into getting there. But I've started in plenty of time, and I don't have to finish this week. I'll set some goals for myself, starting with my résumé—I'll type it up this weekend and then ask my guidance counselor to take a look next week."

Ultimately, the key is to continue to work with children to help them develop their leadership skills. Remember, the work adults (especially parents) do with children to guide them will ultimately determine what types of leaders they will be.

4

Writing Is the Foundation of Great Communication

For many kids, thanks to writers ranging from Dr. Seuss to J.K. Rowling, reading can be a lot of fun…but writing is hard work! And what's more, I believe (as do many teachers) that writing is becoming more difficult to teach. That's because—technically—writing is a much more prevalent part of our daily lives than it has ever been before. Think about it: We're constantly communicating with one another via text, instant messaging, and email. These days, many kids grow up clutching some electronic device or other from infancy onward!

Here's the problem: This new type of writing is short, abbreviated, and almost a language in and of itself. It's not unusual for me to have to ask my kids to decipher some of the texting lingo they use, like TTYL (talk to you later), IDK (I don't know), and JIC (just in case). To children who are used to this space-saving jargon, writing in full and complete sentences can be like writing in a foreign language! Therein

To children who are used to this space-saving jargon, writing in full and complete sentences can be like writing in a foreign language!

lies the first difficulty in teaching young people the art of effective and appropriate writing.

To compound the problem, our society doesn't hold writing in as high esteem as it does other academic areas. I hear parents complaining that some of their children do not enjoy or are not excelling in their math and science classes, but I rarely hear them say that their kids don't possess a command of the written English language. Yes, we all know that writing skills can lead to better grades and greater academic achievement, but we also tend to believe that once you leave high school or college, your grades hold little importance.

If an adult isn't a good writer, he or she is likely to say something along the lines of, "Well, I'm just not good with words. It is what it is." There's usually no attempt to improve in this area, either—maybe because most people assume that unless they're authors, journalists, or the like, they'll never really benefit from being able to write well—or lose out because they aren't comfortable wielding words. They don't realize that of all the academic skills that are judged and graded in school, writing may matter the most.

Writing IS Important—Here's Why!

My marketing consulting firm has been studying the companies with which we work for the past decade, and we consistently find that only one in five people typically feel that they can write. Not coincidentally, these self-identified writers are often the ones who rise to the top of their firms. Believe it or not, writing is a skill for which some hiring firms are desperate. After all, writing is the key to getting ideas across, compelling people to act, marketing a product or service, and presenting a firm professionally.

A Growing Shortage...of Writers!

A summary of a study published in *Personnel Update* states: "Writing skills...of executives are shockingly low, indicating that schools and colleges dismally fail with at least two-thirds of the people who pass through the education pipeline who are unable to write a simple letter." And the need for workers with writing skills will only increase. The U.S. Department of Labor has indicated that most future jobs will require writing skills.

Think about it this way: Organizations, from bakeries to brokerage firms, are not looking for employees who can text barely recognizable words in a matter of seconds. While it's nice (and even valuable) to be able to quickly text something like, "r u picking up the kids?" to your spouse instead of having a five-minute conversation to the same effect, you're not going to be communicating in this way at work. In a professional setting, Net lingo is not helping us to communicate *better*—just more quickly and more frequently. And if you pepper your emails and memos with texting slang on a regular basis, you'll find that you quickly lose respect and professional credibility. It's easy to see why potential employers care very much about writing skills and complain when they're given only applicants who are poor writers. The bottom line is, in business, quality communication is much more valuable than speedy communication.

Net lingo is not helping us to communicate *better*—just more quickly and more frequently.

While my personal area of expertise is the business world, I know that the benefits of being a good writer don't stop in the boardroom. Being able to communicate through the written word can have a profound impact on all areas of an individual's life, from relationship building to personal development and more.

Consider this: Marquette University's Writing Center (which focuses on helping students develop their writing skills) has posted numerous reasons why writing is so important. The following information is also echoed in brochures from both Brown University and the University of Missouri:

What Makes Writing So Important?

- Writing is the primary basis upon which your work, your learning, and your intellect will be judged—in college, in the workplace, and in the community.
- Writing expresses who you are as a person.
- Writing is portable and permanent. It makes your thinking visible.
- Writing helps you move easily among facts, inferences, and opinions without getting confused—and without confusing your reader.
- Writing promotes your ability to pose worthwhile questions.
- Writing fosters your ability to explain a complex position to readers, and to yourself.
- Writing helps others give you feedback.
- Writing helps you refine your ideas when you give others feedback.
- Writing requires that you anticipate your readers' needs. Your ability to do so demonstrates your intellectual flexibility and maturity.
- Writing ideas down preserves them so that you can reflect upon them later.
- Writing out your ideas permits you to evaluate the adequacy

of your argument.

- Writing stimulates you to extend a line of thought beyond your first impressions or gut responses.
- Writing helps you understand how truth is established in a given discipline.
- Writing equips you with the communication and thinking skills you need to participate effectively in a democracy.
- Writing is an essential job skill.

Clearly, helping your child to develop strong writing skills is a worthwhile investment that will pay dividends long after youth has been left behind. A good writer stands out, and that's what we all want for our kids—to be noticed, appreciated, and hired. So, what can you do as a parent to help your kids become good writers? Here are some effective starting points.

Readers Become Writers

Reading and writing development are intertwined (especially in early learning). So when you encourage your children to read (or when you read to them if they're young), you're also helping them to become better writers.

If you've watched interviews of authors or been to book talks, you may have noticed that these individuals had something in common: Almost all professional writers say that they are also voracious readers. What's more, most writers say that they've had their noses in books since they were children. That's not a coincidence. When you regularly expose yourself to good (or at least publish-worthy) writing, you unconsciously begin to absorb difficult-to-teach concepts like how a compelling argument is constructed, what makes for good flow, and how words can be used to tap into emotions, to name just a few. You begin to develop a sense of what "works" and what doesn't. And the more writing you're exposed to, the more your vocabulary (and your comfort level with using it) will grow.

When you encourage your children to read, you're also helping them to become better writers.

I'll admit that relatively few children will grow up to earn their salaries solely through using the written word. But as we've already established, individuals in almost all lines of work can benefit from being able to write effectively and persuasively. And if good reading begets good writing, it makes sense to keep kids reading long past the days that they struggle through *Run, Spot, Run*.

Encourage your kids to "learn from the masters" by reading throughout their pre-teen and teen years. You might consider giving them books (or bookstore gift cards) as gifts, allowing them to stay up later to read, or coming up with a rewards system for books read. (For example, X number of parent-approved books read per month earns a trip out for pizza and ice cream.)

For younger kids, take turns reading chapters in a book to one another. You may be surprised by how beloved this tradition becomes! And by the way, reading aloud is not just for kids. Actually, it's a time-honored tradition. In the Victorian era, for example, it was customary for a family member to read aloud every evening, with children and adults alike listening intently to the story. (Okay, it sounds old-fashioned, but give it a try—you just might like it!)

Use Games to Build Vocabulary

A rich vocabulary is the foundation for good, in-depth writing—so play games that will build your child's vocabulary. Classic choices are Scrabble, Wheel of Fortune, and Hangman. If your child prefers a solitary activity, word searches and crosswords are also quite effective. Nowadays, most of these games can be found online, so take advantage of technology. (I've said before that it doesn't always have to take away from the quality of communication!) Especially if your child is older and tech-savvy, she can even download vocab-boosting apps like Words with Friends on her smartphone.

> A rich vocabulary is the foundation for good, in-depth writing.

Once your child adds a new word to her arsenal, encourage her to use it—and be sure to acknowledge that you've noticed and that you're proud when she does!

Train the Mind

In their book *The Well-Trained Mind*, authors Jessie Wise and Susan Wise Bauer share a writing process for elementary students that reinforces good writing habits and that will even help older children who are having trouble with spelling and punctuation. Here's a quick run-down:

- **For younger kids: Copywork.** When kids are learning the basics of writing, they often struggle with "basics" that are second-nature to adults, such as remembering to capitalize certain letters, to put spaces between words, and to punctuate their sentences. Copying a brief selection directly from a book (perhaps just a two- or three-word sentence to start) will allow your child to *see* what a sentence is supposed to look like as he's writing it himself, thus reinforcing both visual and motor memory. Once your child has finished his copywork, look over it with him and compare his writing to the original.

Talk about any differences you see, and be sure to praise him for everything he did accurately.

- **For older kids: Dictation practice.** By the time most children reach second or third grade, they have mastered the "basics" of writing and can do copywork accurately. Now it's time to move on to dictation. In this exercise, you will read a selection aloud—perhaps from a book or newspaper article. Ask your child to write as accurately as possible what she hears, and remind her to apply what she has learned about spacing, punctuation, etc. (Again, this will reinforce what she knows about sentence and paragraph structure.) At first, your child may be able to remember only one sentence at a time, and that's okay. Your ultimate goal is to gradually add more and more to her memory—another skill that will serve her well in life! As with copywork, be sure to help your child review what she wrote. Talk about what she did well and identify what she might be able to improve next time.

Take Every Opportunity to Write

As your child begins to read and build her vocabulary, encourage her to put what she's learning to use. Here are some ways to incorporate writing into your child's life:

- **Be a stickler about her school writing assignments.** Kids usually start having basic "writing homework" in the very early grades. It's best if you can get involved from the very beginning. Always try to look at her writing homework before she turns it in. Don't do it for her, obviously (that would defeat the purpose!), but when she does something that is incorrect or lackluster or doesn't flow logically, engage her in a conversation about it.

    "Can you see that there's no transition between paragraph three and paragraph four? See that you're writing about the meteor shower and then you jump immediately to the dead dinosaur. Maybe you need a few sentences that explain HOW the meteors may have killed the dinosaur..." (Then, brainstorm with her on how to make the transition.)

    Or, "See that you used the word 'good' five times in your essay about homemade ice cream. Surely there are some better, more creative words to use to describe the ice cream." (Then, help her brainstorm words like: refreshing, chilly, rich, delicious, sugary.)

    Many kids (and adults!) are lazy. They will do the minimum amount of work they can get away with. Don't let your child develop lazy writing habits, no matter how much she protests and rolls her eyes. The earlier you can help her understand what good writing looks like, and get her in the habit of working on her writing homework until it's good, the better foundation she'll have to build from later on.

- **Ask your child to make a case.** Whenever your child wants something—whether it's a new bicycle or a later bedtime—encourage him to list the reasons why he wants what he does, and then ask him to make his case to you in writing. (The older your child is, the better this method works!) I have found that when my children are able to present to me a well-structured argument for wanting or needing something, they often get it. (For a good example, see my daughter's story in Chapter 8 about putting together a PowerPoint presentation aimed at getting a second dog. To make a long story short, our family now includes two canines.) This exercise is great practice for later in your child's life, too. Demanding and begging rarely work in our house—and it won't work on your child's future teachers, professors, and employers, either!

- **Encourage your child to keep a journal.** If your child is naturally introspective, you might not need to use much persuasion. If he'd rather be outside or watching TV than scribbling in a notebook, ask him to start by describing your family's recent vacation, for example, or perhaps his experiences at summer camp or on a recent field trip. This exercise will take only fifteen minutes, but over time, your child might just unwittingly develop a taste for writing (and he'll enjoy looking back on his recorded memories). If your child is in his teens, you might alternatively encourage him to start a blog about something that interests him.

- **Insist on written invitations and thank-you notes.** Whether your child is inviting her friends to her birthday sleepover or writing thank-you notes for gifts she's received, ask her to do the writing herself. You can look over her work and give her pointers for improvement; e.g., *Be sure to describe what you'll be doing at the party* or *Tell Grandma what you've been drawing with the paint set she gave you.*

- **Consider helping her find a pen pal.** If you thought the idea of pen pals was obsolete, think again. While it's true that the Internet has made it less likely that kids will go the old-fashioned "pen and paper/wait by the mailbox" route, there are plenty of websites that allow for high-tech correspondence. Yes, you need to monitor your child's correspondence, but having a pen pal provides plenty of practice for written self-expression. Besides, it's a great chance for him to meet kids from other cultures as well as those who share his interests.

- **Introduce your children to business writing.** If your child is old enough (most likely a tween or a teen), ask him to brainstorm what his dream job might be and then let him do a little online research as to what qualifications a competitive applicant might possess. Next, help him put together a résumé and cover letter as though he were actually applying. Focus on highlighting relevant skills and writing persuasively. (Or, if your teen is older, help him to do this for a real part-time or summer job.) It's never too early to introduce your children to concepts that many adults struggle with well into their careers!

- **Help your children post reviews.** If your child has read a new book or received a new toy, for example, suggest that she write a review to post on a website like Amazon! Help her to think through what she likes and doesn't like about the object being reviewed, and explain why other visitors to the website will find her opinions valuable. She'll love seeing her review "published"—and she'll also feel a sense of accomplishment because her writing is helpful to others.

- **Put the kibosh on "K THX." (Translation: Ban Internet slang.)** Don't allow your kids to abbreviate outside of texting, at least when you're the recipient. I'll warn you: This is one of those rules that, when instituted, might brand you as a "mean" mom or dad. But trust me—you'll ultimately be doing your kids a favor. The next time your teen sends you an email saying she'll TTYL, reply back asking her to spell out all of those words (and encourage her to do the same in emails to others!).

Simple Tips for Becoming a Better Writer

If your child is beginning to see writing as "fun" and not "drudgery," share any or all of the following eight tips with her to help her improve!

1. Create an outline of your idea, your reinforcing points, and your conclusion.
2. Keep the subject matter concise—shorter is better as long as you clearly make your points.
3. Start and end strong—hook them in the beginning and leave them fulfilled yet wanting more of your writing when they get to the end.
4. Read great writers—their style will help you learn yourself.
5. Write frequently, because the more you write, the better you will be.
6. Eliminate distractions so you will be able to focus and let your ideas flow from your mind to the paper.
7. Read your material aloud to see if it sounds as good as you think.
8. Get feedback!

Ultimately, writing doesn't have to be as difficult as we often make it out to be. When you help your child to connect his writing with a measurable outcome, he'll see how useful and effective it is…and he'll have a head start down a path that many people avoid even as adults.

5

Speaking Effectively to Individuals and Groups

Right now you may be reading the title of this chapter and thinking, *Hmmm. Isn't Maribeth talking about two different things? Surely a lunch conversation with, say, a business associate isn't the same thing as presenting in front of a group.*

This is a common belief. But I am here to tell you that speaking is speaking is speaking. (And I say this as someone who regularly speaks one-on-one with clients and spends maybe 100 days a year speaking in front of groups.) Anything more formal than a gossip session with your lifelong best friend— that is, any conversation that has a goal—should have the same thought and preparation put into it as a public speech. What's more (and I'll discuss this later on in the chapter), good presentations come across as one-on-one conversations.

All that said, the ability to speak effectively is a powerful life skill. You may have noticed: The way you speak greatly influences the way other people treat you. If you talk softly, mumble your words, or are fearful of speaking to others, you'll give the person to whom you're speaking the impression that you don't care—even if that couldn't be farther from the truth. However, if you speak with confidence, you foster a completely different—and significantly better—image and perception of yourself. Whether in a personal interaction, in school, or (eventually) in business, your speaking style can drastically impact how much others respect you and how well they remember you.

Whether in a personal interaction, in school, or (eventually) in business, your speaking style can drastically impact how much others respect you and how well they remember you.

That said, changing your speaking style can be *much* easier said than done. Did you know that the fear of public speaking outranks even the fear of death? That's a pretty big barrier to overcome! And unfortunately, our children might be at an added disadvantage when it comes to rising above this already common fear. After all, our new technologically advanced society teaches us to use computers much more efficiently than it does to speak. In fact, many schools *require* students to take some sort of computer-skills course, while public speaking is offered as an elective (if at all).

The problem is, that doesn't reflect the real world at all. First of all, not all careers are built on computer use, but speaking (public and otherwise) is an essential requirement for professionals in *all* walks of life. Throughout our lives, any one of us might be asked to give a presentation, train someone, or just share our ideas with colleagues or potential clients.

Those Who Speak Well Win!

It's a good idea for us as parents to accustom our children as early as possible to conveying their thoughts clearly and effectively in a public setting—the benefits they'll reap are likely to grow throughout their lives.

As you know, great communicators are able to command respect, get their ideas across quickly, and accomplish what they set out to do. They can also develop a sense of a personal connection with people whom they have never met—nor will ever meet—one-on-one. The truth is, individuals who can speak effectively to individuals *and* to groups are more likely to advance to higher positions—that's why good speakers run many of the largest companies in the world and are our political leaders.

In his book *The Exceptional Presenter*, author Timothy Koegel refers to the Corporate Recruiters Survey that is published every year by the Graduate Management Admission Council and is reported in the *Wall Street Journal*. The survey ranks business schools based on the impressions that corporate recruiters have of their MBA students. These recruiters rated the students on twenty-one different attributes. And the attribute that the recruiters (89 percent of them, to be exact) considered to be the most important one for a student to possess was "Communication/Interpersonal Skills."

"People who possess exceptional communication skills maintain a distinct competitive advantage in winning new business and securing the best jobs," says Koegel, a presentation and media consultant in Washington, D.C. "In an unforgiving economy, their advantage becomes even more pronounced."[v]

People who possess exceptional communication skills maintain a distinct competitive advantage.

Koegel's observation is extremely relevant to a chapter on speaking because the principles for building valuable relationships and connecting in a meaningful way with clients are the very same principles used by the great speakers who connect with their audiences. Mastering the art of speaking means becoming the embodiment of connection; and a prolific speaker takes *all* connecting principles and weaves them together in a short period of time. During a presentation, the audience connects emotionally with the speaker and can be inspired to take some action because of the information conveyed.

v Koegel, Timothy. *The Exceptional Presenter: A Proven Formula to Open Up and Own the Room.* Austin: Greenleaf Book Group Press, 2007.

The Importance of Early Learning

Over the years I have brought my daughter and son with me (separately) on business trips during the summer when I could and when it was appropriate. When my daughter, Elizabeth, was ten years old, I recall her engaging a whole table of business professionals at a dinner meeting of about twenty people during a convention. I was engaged in a conversation, and Lizzie found herself being asked questions by individuals at another table. Initially oblivious, I glanced up when I heard laughter coming from that other table. I was shocked to see Lizzie seemingly delivering a presentation complete with laugh lines. I found

I was shocked to see Lizzie seemingly delivering a presentation complete with laugh lines.

out later that she was telling some stories about ME (of all people!), which others found quite amusing…especially since they related to my driving skills.

Lizzie's storytelling was all in fun, of course, but I was truly amazed at and proud of how effectively my daughter had engaged a group of adults. The individuals at that table came up to me later to share how entertaining and engaging Lizzie had been. Yes, I know I'm her mother, but I do feel compelled to point out that Lizzie is not a ham or someone who is always seeking attention, just someone who, when given the right opportunity, is able to keep herself and others engaged and amused. Because of that attribute, I'm sure that Lizzie has a very "connected" future ahead of her! Here's why:

If you ask a well-spoken adult when she started speaking so effectively, she will likely share that when she was a child, her parents (or other adults in her life) frequently encouraged her to talk or tell stories to her friends. In fact, research shows that this driving force—encouragement—is a common occurrence.

Serena Greenslade, ANEA (Associate of New Era Academy of Speech and Drama), has written a powerful guide titled *Helping Children to Speak*. Greenslade, from Dorset, England, is a teacher and certified speech trainer (certified with a teaching diploma in speech training in the UK). In her guide, she shares the benefits of helping children to speak clearly and confidently:

- Children who can speak clearly and confidently are happy children.
- Children who can speak clearly and confidently are more likely to be at the top of their class because they're not frightened to speak or ask the teacher questions.
- Children who can speak clearly and confidently are willing to join in at social events— parties, clubs, sports, etc. They don't need to have a parent with them all the time because they can speak for themselves.
- Children who can speak clearly and confidently are successful children.
- Confident, successful children sleep well at night.

Start Early (Before They Develop the Fear)

Believe it or not, people are not necessarily *born* with a fear of public speaking. In fact, if children learn speech and presentation skills early on, they may never have to experience this phobia for themselves. Again, we're back to "easier said than done"—with good reason! Many parents with whom I've spoken wonder how they could possibly train their children to become confident speakers since they themselves also struggle in this area. The good news is, I don't believe that there is a complex science to the training. You simply need to show your kids that they

> **If children learn speech and presentation skills early on, they may never have to experience this phobia for themselves.**

can communicate with others through words, and that doing this will help them achieve their goals.

Chapter 7 of this book contains numerous suggestions for encouraging your child to speak to both individuals and groups in real-world settings. In addition, I will share a few practical tips here that will help your children to improve their speaking skills:

- **Get some practice.** The easiest way to integrate speaking into your child's life is to give him opportunities to practice doing so. I've found that one of the best (and often, least intimidating) ways to help your child improve his speaking is to ask him to read out loud. My neighbor does this daily with her children—she will read one chapter, and her child will read the next. This method not only builds reading skills but also confidence in speaking. (And if you keep a dictionary close by to look up unfamiliar words, it will also build vocabulary!)

- **Recount the day.** Finally, a great speaking lesson can start when your child returns home each day from school. It's common for parents to ask, "So, what did you do today?" And it's also common for children to respond with a mumbled, "Nothing," or, "Not much." Don't let your youngster get away that easy! From start to finish, get him in the habit of describing *in detail* the things that happened throughout his day. Be sure to give your child your full attention—and appropriate responses—during this recital!

- **Get outside your comfort zone.** Exposing your child to new ideas and individuals is a good idea for many reasons—and improving her speaking skills is one of them! Think about it this way: It's fairly easy to talk to someone whom you know well and like. It's much more challenging—and growth-inspiring—to converse with someone with whom you don't know well and might not have much in common with. You must think much more carefully about how to engage the other person.

- **Play Show and Tell.** We normally think of Show and Tell as a game that is played at school—but it's also a powerful tool that can easily be integrated at home. Have your child begin by giving impromptu Show and Tell presentations for family and friends. My favorite examples of this are to ask your child to do a Show and Tell about his very favorite things, the gifts he received for a holiday or birthday, or a new skill he has acquired. Invite people to listen in. Eventually, you can ask your child to practice in advance. Be sure to compliment him on his preparation and cheer him on during his great performance!

  If your child is older (a tween or teen), you can "update" Show and Tell by creating a game to be played as a family or at other social gatherings. Ask your child to engage an adult in order to recount a story from a recent trip, for example, or about an achievement at school. Each time your tween or teen engages an adult, he gets a point… which he can then trade in for a pre-determined reward.

- **Stage a public performance.** If your child is willing, encourage her to participate in theatre, debate, or forensics (public speaking). When a child or young adult acts in public or recites poetry or other prose in a competition format, she will likely develop into a confident speaker. Serena Greenslade notes that signing your child up for a drama class is also a great way for her to learn voice projection, memorization, managing stage fright, and using tools like props and visuals to strengthen the force of her words. You'll find that in addition to developing your child's natural talents, public performance will build a sense of accomplishment and confidence, which is most valuable of all!

- **Join a club.** Joining a school club is another effective way for your child to develop public speaking skills (and perhaps also make some new friends who share a common interest!). Drama clubs, debate clubs, junior toastmasters, and science clubs are just some of the student clubs that give children the opportunity to speak and give demonstrations in a public setting.

- **Choose to present.** Don't look at school presentations as "just" an assignment—help your child to see them as an opportunity! Help him to think about his approach and the information he wants to include. (I'll talk about effective techniques in the next section.) Challenge him to truly pique the curiosity of his teacher and classmates, and have him practice his delivery at home with you. Also, if your child is given a choice between completing a written report, a diorama, or a presentation, for example, encourage him to choose the presentation—it will still involve and utilize his writing skills, and it will also give him a chance to polish his ability to speak to a group.

Encouraging the Introvert

Many children will take to speaking in front of groups like ducks to water. But others—introverts especially—will find that being the center of public attention isn't easy or enjoyable. I will talk more about how to encourage introverts to communicate in a later chapter, but here are a few presentation-specific tips if your child prefers silence over speaking:

- **Work with her one-on-one.** It's a good idea to help any child improve her speaking skills one-on-one, but introverts especially will appreciate and thrive on personal attention and help.

- **Practice in front of family.** Before the "big day" (whether it's in class, at church, or at a club meeting), ask your child to practice her presentation in front of your family or others with whom she is comfortable.

- **Record her speech.** We are often our own worst critics. Chances are, your child thinks that her ability to present is much worse than is really the case. During a practice session at home, record her speech, then play it back to her. She'll probably be surprised by how great she sounds!

Preparing a Presentation

Presentations are a standard element of school assignments—but your child won't leave them behind once she receives a diploma. While not all professions will require employees to give formal presentations, everyone is required from time to time to present an opinion or to convince another person to change his or her mind. For all intents and purposes, these endeavors can be seen as presentations too.

While your child is young, teach her the basic building blocks of a powerful presentation. I have found that there are three distinct sections of such a presentation, whether it lasts five minutes or an entire day. The older your child is, the more she'll be able to understand and utilize the "Challenge-Solution-Call to Action" method, but even younger kids can be taught the basics.

- Address the **challenge.**
- Form your **solution.**
- Give the audience a **call to action.**

It's a Conversation, Not a Presentation

Once your child has begun to understand and utilize how to effectively structure a presentation, he'll have taken the first step toward becoming an effective speaker. But there's another piece to this puzzle: delivery. Especially if you have a tween or a teen, talk together about any speech you might hear, whether it's a sermon or a graduation address. You'll find that most speakers will deliver a highly scripted presentation. However,

> **Great speakers seem to have a *conversation* with their audience.**

the great speakers—despite how well planned, organized, and structured their talks may appear—seem to have a *conversation* with their audience.

Think about it—if you're speaking to an audience of one or two—in other words, having a conversation—you wouldn't likely stand and deliver a formal presentation if your aim was to be compelling. It would seem odd.

So why then, when there are many people gathered, do many speakers change their approach? In front of a large group, I've found that a speaker's cadence may change as he or she morphs into a "presenter" who is performing, instead of someone connecting through a genuine exchange.

Veteran motivational humorist Lou Heckler—who has delivered thousands of keynote speeches for corporations, trade associations, and universities—also coaches other speakers. "Audiences want to believe you know more than they do about a certain topic—that's why they've come to hear you speak," Heckler says. "But they also want to feel you are, in some ways, one of them." Heckler shares that seasoned speakers apply three proven techniques when they really want to connect with their audiences. Go over them with your teen when it's time for a presentation in order to help him be "real" instead of falling into a role.

"The Heckler Techniques" for Authentic, Conversational Speaking

- **Speak to an audience of one.** Regardless of whether you're speaking to five people or 3,500 people, use a style that feels like you're really just talking to one person. Instead of sweeping your eyes across the audience like you're an animated mannequin in a department store window, look at individuals and move from one to another with a certain amount of deliberation. Visualize that you're talking to a treasured friend.

- **Think of your talk as a dialogue, not a monologue.** Recognize that audience members will be reacting—even if it's subconsciously—to everything that you say. Don't rush things. Utilize strategic pauses to give them time to consider what you've just said. Watch and observe how TV game show hosts ask the contestant a question, listen to the answer, and then pause a few moments before telling the contestant whether he or she is right or wrong. They're inviting the viewing audience to "participate" mentally. You can do the same thing with periodic pauses in your speech.

- **Use some rhetorical questions.** Pepper your observations in a talk with phrases like, "Isn't this something you've noticed?" or, "Am I the only one who gets frustrated when...?" It invites the audience members to think about what you've said and connect it to a similar experience in their lives. It makes them think, *Hey, he/she knows what I go through each day.*

I've had the good fortune to hear some of the best business speakers in the world through my work and also as a member of the National Speakers Association, and I've observed one significant difference between some of the greats and everyone else: The most prolific speakers are able to connect with their audiences immediately, build rapport in seconds, and are able to hold this connection throughout an entire presentation. They engage their audiences from beginning to end. And the great news is, this can be done successfully at any age with practice and the development of confidence. It is a skill that truly will last a lifetime.

6

The Quiet Child: Introversion, Shyness, and Relationship Development

Some children are natural "chatterboxes." They'll talk to anyone about anything at any time (even if you'd rather they kept quiet sometimes!). They have no fear of approaching others and interacting with them, and what's more, they're good at it and seem to actually thrive on being the center of attention.

With other children, though, it's just the opposite. Whether they're in elementary school or high school, some kids avoid the spotlight whenever possible. They are more solitary and prefer to interact with people they know and are comfortable with. They might also seem (to outsiders, anyway) to be "socially awkward," "quiet," or "not confident."

If this describes your child, he or she may be shy, may be an introvert...or may be both. And that's okay! Despite what many people assume, shyness can be overcome. And introverted children can be the greatest connectors of all because of the special gifts that they possess. These individuals, no matter their age, are not "flawed" and do not need to be "fixed"—they simply communicate and connect differently from those who are outgoing or extroverted. (Think of extroverts and introverts as pianos and trumpets. Both can make beautiful music, and neither is "less than" the other because it is different—they must simply be operated in different ways in order to produce a melody.)

Introverted children can be the greatest connectors of all because of the special gifts that they possess.

To avoid confusion I'd like to briefly discuss the differences between "shy" and "introverted" prior to going into more detail about each—because although the two words are often used as synonyms, they're *not* necessarily the same thing. In fact, being shy has little to do with being an introvert. Shyness is characterized by an element of anxiety and apprehension that prevents an individual from interacting as he would like to. Meanwhile, an introvert is simply a person who is more energized by being alone than by being around other people. An introvert may avoid a social situation because it drains his energy, not because he is afraid of interaction with others.

In other words, while an introvert may also be shy, introversion itself is not shyness.

The bottom line is, it's a challenge to raise a child who has confidence in building and cultivating relationships with others whether she's an extrovert or introvert. (Believe it or not, statistics say that there are actually more shy extroverts than shy introverts!) The key as a parent is to properly identify your child's type and then guide and encourage her so that she learns to cultivate relationship skills appropriately. Whether your child is extroverted, introverted, or shy, pushing her into a "connecting mold" she doesn't fit into can undermine her confidence and result in years of unproductive communications and interactions with others. In this chapter I hope to give you the knowledge and tools to make sure that *doesn't* happen.

> **Pushing your child into a "connecting mold" she doesn't fit into can result in years of unproductive communications and interactions with others.**

The Shy Child

First, I'd like to discuss shy children. *Merriam-Webster's Dictionary* defines a shy individual as someone who is easily frightened, timid, exercises avoidance with people, and is hesitant in committing oneself. Someone who is shy holds himself aloof from others because various types of social interactions cause him to feel anxious or afraid, not because he would rather be alone. In other words, an introverted child simply has less desire to be around other people, whereas a shy child *wants* to socialize but feels uncomfortable doing so. Introverts can socialize effectively when they want to; shy children cannot simply "switch off" their apprehension and nerves.

Figuring out which side of the line your child falls on can be difficult (especially for younger children who might be unable to dissect or articulate their feelings), but close observance over time can show you whether your child withdraws because of preference or fear. (In some cases, perhaps it's both.) If your child repeatedly tells you that she wishes she had more friends, for example, or that she is scared to talk to people, there is a strong chance she is suffering from shyness.

Nothing robs a talented person of opportunity more than shyness.

Obviously, being shy can greatly limit your child's opportunities. In fact, nothing robs a talented person of opportunity more than shyness—but the good news is, this hurdle isn't permanent.

The Technology Connection

As I've alluded to before in this book, I believe that today's world is cultivating shyness and enabling those who already suffer from it. In other words, an over-reliance on technology is stunting many children's social growth. Think about it: It's easier than ever to refrain from facing our fears because a great deal of face-to-face communication can be avoided through the use of technology. This is especially true for the current generation of children, many of whom learned to type and text while learning to read!

It's important for parents to realize that people in general aren't nearly as shy when texting or chatting online. Kids (and many adults!) will type things they would never have the courage to say face-to-face to the same person. Again, I'm not saying that technology is inherently *bad*, but I do believe that it can prevent children from getting over their fears of interacting in a variety of social settings. "Hiding" online doesn't set anyone up to be optimally productive, happy, and successful.

Renée Gilbert, Ph.D., a licensed clinical psychologist and frequent media contributor, teaches classes on parenting shy children. She instructs parents to avoid labeling their children and highlighting shyness as a child's defining characteristic. Instead, when introducing your obviously shy child, say something like, "Sarah's a little shy when she first meets people, but you should see her dance. Wow!" or, "I guess John takes after Albert Einstein. He was shy too, you know. But they both have an incredible passion for science."

Putting a positive spin on the fear may make it less of a noticeable stigma in the eyes of your child, which is an important first step in overcoming it. Gilbert also says to stack the cards in your child's favor by teaching social skills early and often. Without role modeling, breaking the shyness cycle might be more difficult.

Shyness Isn't Just for Kids

Gilbert makes a point of telling parents that shyness isn't something that only kids experience; in fact, 50 percent of adults are shy, too. If you fall into this category, it may be difficult for you to model confident social interactions to your children. Push yourself to overcome this fear yourself! That might start with small things like saying "hi" to someone first, proactively complimenting others often, and simply putting yourself and your child in social situations.

Reducing Nervous Nerves

In addition to helping your child not be defined by her shyness, good preparation will reduce her nervous feelings when speaking face-to-face by almost 75 percent and will increase the likelihood of avoiding errors to 95 percent (Source: Fred Pryor Organization). That's exactly why I included the Teachable Moments section of this book (Chapter 7)—to provide invaluable tools and strategies for helping kids gain confidence through rehearsal and preparation. In addition, here are a few ways you can help your shy child to become more socially confident:

- **Work on self-confidence.** Many people (children *and* adults!) fear social interaction because consciously or unconsciously they think that they are inadequate, not interesting, or unable to hold up their end of the conversation. Always take every opportunity to point out your child's strengths and praise her when she succeeds—*especially* in a social setting!

- **Curiously listen.** I cover curious listening in-depth in Chapter 2. Helping your shy child to develop this skill can lessen his social apprehension. If he is truly focused on hearing and understanding the other person, he will be *less* aware of his own discomfort. And over time, he'll realize that he is successfully connecting...and his shyness will begin to dissipate.

- **Make a script.** If you know that a social interaction is going to take place beforehand, write a basic conversation script with your child. Knowing what to expect might not erase the fear of interacting, but it *can* erase the fear of the unknown. For example, if your daughter is going to meet your sister's new husband for the first time, suggest that she say, "Hello. My name is Anne. I am your new niece!"

- **Banish perfectionism.** Many shy individuals latch onto conversational stumbles or stutters and blow their importance out of proportion. Some kids may dwell for hours on an awkward pause in the conversation or a stammered joke that fell flat. To help him realize that it's okay not to be perfect, just switch on a television program that is taped live. Eventually, most presenters and interviewers will make a speech "mistake." Point it out to your child, and then help him to realize that the occasional error doesn't make the program any less effective or enjoyable.

As is the case with developing any skill set, proceed slowly, one step at a time, and always stay encouraging! And again, be sure to avoid defining your child as "shy."

The Introverted Child

Often confused with shy individuals, introverts are simply wired to experience the world differently from the majority who are extroverts. In brief, introverts are typically introspective and reflective individuals, but unless they are also shy, they do not *fear* social interaction—they just don't find it as necessary as extroverts and usually prefer to remain alone or in small groups. It's often difficult for extroverts to understand, but introverts feel drained by a great deal of social interaction and need to be alone to "recharge" their batteries. (For extroverts, it's just the opposite. Outgoing folks thrive on attention and interaction and dislike being by themselves.) Because of these key differences, introverts have their own unique set of strengths, which influences their connecting style.

In her book *The Hidden Gifts of the Introverted Child*, author Marti Olsen Laney, Psy.D., offers insight into introverts and gives parents valuable advice. Here, I'd like to share what Olsen Laney identifies as some of the characteristics that are shared by most introverts. Introverts:

> Often confused with shy individuals, introverts are simply wired to experience the world differently from the majority who are extroverts.

- Enter new situations slowly
- Speak softly and sometimes hunt for words
- Need time alone to recharge
- Have one or two good friends

To learn more about the characteristics of introverts—as well as to determine whether or not your child might be one—take Olsen Laney's quiz located at http://www.myparentime. com/articles/06/articleS591.shtml.

You might also consider using the Myers-Briggs Type Indicator. It is an assessment that can help you learn about your child's personality type in much more detail—specifically, how she processes information and most effectively communicates. This type of knowledge can improve your relationship with each other and enable you to better prepare your child to connect and lead. For more information about how the MBTI relates to children, visit http://old.kidzmet. com/content_pages/view/MBTI.

The Successful Introvert

At first glance, a list of introvert characteristics might dismay parents. After all, our society tends to define successful individuals as being outgoing, popular, charismatic, and high-energy. However, don't make the mistake of thinking that because your child is an introvert, she is doomed to live her life in the shadow of her outgoing peers. Quite the opposite might be the case, actually! Before I talk about how you can encourage your introvert to connect, I'd like to show you just how effective the introvert's style of connecting can be.

Consider this: Introverts make up about 60 percent of the intellectually gifted population but only about 25 to 40 percent of the general population. By and large, that's because introverts are naturally thoughtful, observant, creative, and self-motivated people.

Aside from predisposing them to be identified as gifted, these qualities also mean that introverts have the potential to be *better* communicators than their extroverted peers! Think about it: To be an engaging person, you don't necessarily need to be the type of person who loves to socialize, attend big parties, and network whenever you get the chance. You simply need to make strong, genuine connections with individuals— and that's an introvert's specialty since she prefers to focus on one person at a time, likes to listen quite a bit, and is very detail-oriented.

Recently, one of the nation's best-known networking professionals came to the realization that he is an introvert!

Ivan Misner, Ph.D., founder of BNI and the author of eleven books on networking, shared with me that he recently discovered that he is actually an introvert. *What?* Misner said that his wife of twenty years told him during dinner one night that he displayed many introvert tendencies. Misner was shocked! How could a professional speaker and the founder of the largest business networking organization in the world be an introvert?

Curious, Misner took an online test and discovered that his wife was right—at least partially. Turns out, he is a "situational extrovert," meaning that he is reserved around strangers but very outgoing in the right context.

"It struck me why I started BNI," Misner said. "I was naturally uncomfortable meeting new people. BNI created a system that enabled me to meet people in an organized, structured networking environment that did not require that I actually…talk to strangers."

Misner isn't the only introvert to find a way to succeed in business, either. Believe it or not, I've noticed that introverts often make the best salespeople. Surprised? I was too, at first. Then I realized that most people picture salespeople as being extroverts: chatty, in-your-face, high-energy people. But in reality, the most effective salespeople don't talk their clients into submission. Instead, they listen. They form meaningful relationships. They notice and understand the feelings of the other party. They figure out what their prospects really want and then position their product or service as the answer.

I could go into much more detail, but the bottom line is this skill set is right up an introvert's alley. And no, I'm not saying that your introvert needs to focus on selling as a profession—I'm simply trying to demonstrate that introverts are not destined to be failures in the business realm. As I have stated elsewhere in this book, listening to what *really* matters to other people and building meaningful relationships with them are necessary skills to have in just about any profession.

Owning Your Child's Introversion

Once again, introversion is not a handicap and does not need to be "gotten over." Instead, parents of introverts need to help their kids use their specific gifts to engage with others. The key is to realize that these strategies will differ from those that are effective with extroverts.

Marti Olsen Laney shares that to help your more introverted child interact socially and develop communication skills, it is best for you to create an introvert-friendly environment as opposed to trying to turn him into an extrovert. To do this, you can mirror some of his behaviors. For instance, don't enter into situations without getting a look at the lay of the land and build time into your schedule to be alone and to recharge your batteries. This will help ensure that your child does not constantly feel like the proverbial round peg being forced into a square hole.

You can be even more proactive by understanding how your child's introvert strengths can help him to connect. Here are some common introvert strengths, as well as why they're worth developing and encouraging:

- **Strength:** *Strong Focus.* Introverts typically prefer to focus on one person at a time rather than interacting with a group.

This is because meaningful interactions and strong bonds are important to them, whereas small talk or "surface" interactions drain their energy. Likewise, introverts tend to delve deeply into a single topic or activity rather than wanting to sample a wide variety.

Using it to connect: Your introvert may never be a social butterfly, true. But if she embraces this gift she will win friends for life because the people with whom she "clicks" will feel valued, respected, and loved. She'll also be able to develop good relationships with teachers, coworkers, bosses, etc. Let your child know that it's okay to have several good friends instead of a broad social circle. You can encourage these kinds of interactions by, for instance, suggesting that she celebrate her birthday by planning a fun girls' day with one good friend instead of hosting a roller-skating party for her entire class (a scenario that would send most introverts screaming in the opposite direction). Or during a holiday dinner, suggest that she focus on making sure Grandpa is comfortable and happy instead of trying to chat equally with everyone.

- **Strength:** *Good Listener.* Introverts typically prefer to listen, learn, and gather information before jumping into a situation or making a decision. They don't feel compelled to be the dominant party in conversations.

  Using it to connect: Introverts are born "curious listeners." While an extrovert might need to remind himself to keep his attention on the other person and not interrupt, these behaviors come naturally to introverts.

Encourage your child to develop this skill even further. Practice by quizzing him as to details that were shared in recent conversations. As I have said before, noticing and remembering details will help your child to determine what's important to others and to develop genuine connections.

- **Strength:** *Observant.* For many of the same reasons that introverts are good listeners, they also tend to be observant. In addition to gathering and considering words, they also notice and interpret body language, facial expressions, and other seemingly small—but possibly relevant—details.

  Using it to connect: If people feel valued and respected when you remember their words, they'll feel even more so when you notice and act on what they *don't* say. Introverts are typically good at reading moods and interpreting others' emotions correctly. If you notice that your child has done this, say something along the lines of, "It was really nice of you to notice that Grandma looked a little sad and ask her how she was doing. She really misses Grandpa, and I know that she really appreciates how much you love her."

- **Strength:** *Introspective.* I have heard it said that while introverts are often alone, they are rarely lonely. That's because most introverts enjoy thinking about ideas, interests, and observations. They also tend to be certain in their opinions once they have reached a conclusion.

Using it to connect: As I've already mentioned, a thoughtful person is a good connector because he rarely speaks without prior consideration. Furthermore, an introspective person generally knows himself well. Think about it—in order to communicate well, it's necessary to know what *you* think, need, and want! When you encourage this quality in your child, you'll help ensure that she won't be easily swayed by "the crowd" or by popular opinion…unless popular opinion has merit! You can encourage your child to develop this quality by bringing up a controversial story you've seen on the news (age-appropriate, of course!). Tell him to think about the issue because you'd like to discuss it more later. This gives your child time to solidify his opinion. After you do revisit the topic, play devil's advocate so that your child can defend his position. Chances are, your introvert will find this type of conversation very fulfilling…and so will you!

- **Strength: *Creative.*** Of course, extroverts can be just as creative as introverts, but it's true that an introvert's tendency toward introspection and focus helps him to turn inward and think uniquely. (Extroverts' creativity is more often manifested outwardly; for example, a speaker mesmerizing a crowd.) Plus, many so-called creative hobbies and professions like art, music, and writing require at least occasional solitude. An introvert finds fulfillment in synthesizing ideas, concepts, and emotions into original works.

Using it to connect: The same creativity that helps introverts capture a compelling image with a camera can make their conversation compelling and often memorable. And don't forget that music, art, writing, and more can communicate just as effectively—if not more so than—conversation. Always be sure to compliment your introvert when you see her creativity shining through. Especially if your child is younger, expose her regularly to various creative outlets like symphony performances, plays, art or photography shows, etc. It is a shame when individuals' talents remain untapped because of a lack of opportunity, so if your child expresses an interest in any creative outlet, allow her to pursue it.

- **Strength: *Problem Solver.*** Again, introverts don't have a monopoly on this quality, but several of their other characteristics—such as introspection, creativity, and strong focus—often give them an edge. In general, introverts are wonderful at generating ideas, while extroverts are good at implementing them.

    Using it to connect: When it comes to connecting, outside-the-box observations, ideas, and solutions are often invaluable. Introverts have the ability to become "thought leaders" because of their ability and desire to look at problems from all angles in order to identify the best outcome. While introverts may not want to connect personally with large groups, they can still positively affect many other people in this way. Again, you can use current events to hone your child's problem-solving ability by asking, "What would you do if you were in this leader's position?" On a more personal level (again, if it's age-appropriate), involve your child in family discussions on topics ranging from your budget to hammering out a new chore-division system. At the least, he'll gain some food for thought—and he may just bring up something the adults hadn't considered!

As you can see, there's no need to fit your introvert into an extrovert mold or to prompt him to try to "compete" with his outgoing peers. He is perfectly suited to connect in a quieter and more thoughtful—but no less effective—way! The key is for your child to possess the skills that allow him to communicate face-to-face when necessary—there is no need for him to talk all the time to anyone who is within earshot.

Ultimately, we as parents should strive to cultivate confidence in our children and help them to overcome social fears, whether they are outgoing or more reserved. (And remember, hiding behind technology will not make it easier for anyone who is socially tentative to overcome his or her anxiety!)

Part II

The Learning Lab— Teaching Connector, Communication, and Relationship Skills During Everyday Interactions

7

Teachable Moments: Your World Is a Learning Lab

"Monkey see, monkey do" is more than just a cute saying—it's how connectors are formed. Practically from the day they're born, your children observe and file away everything you say and do…even if you're not aware of just how close their scrutiny is. Why? Well, kids are looking for cues that will teach them how to behave, communicate, and express their emotions. And the fact is, the example *you* set during their formative years will help to shape the personalities they develop as they grow and begin to navigate the world on their own.

When you think about it that way, it's never too early to start teaching your kids how to connect. Unlike learning how to save money or cook a meal, making real and lasting connections on a day-to-day basis isn't a lesson to learn for use "in the future." It's an important skill set that will help your children navigate the world around them *now*. In fact, it's in the everyday exchanges—the very living of life—when the most effective teaching can and should occur.

When it comes to kids *and* adults, there's truly no substitute for experience. So look at the world around you as one big connecting classroom—your own personal learning lab, so to speak—and take advantage of as many teachable moments as you can. Exposing your kids to new types of interactions, situations, and decisions is the best possible training for "real life" you can give them. Start them out small and let them grow as they become more comfortable and experienced.

As you begin your kids' connecting education, remember that this doesn't need to be a big production. As you go through your day, simply be on the lookout for opportunities to encourage your child to be the main communicator in a variety of situations. From the post office to soccer practice to worship services, there is no shortage of scenarios that will allow your kids to actively connect.

Make no mistake, though—some of these situations will be uncomfortable or difficult for kids at first. Let's face it; it's hard for adults to have uncomfortable conversations, so we can't expect our kids to naturally take to them like they did to chocolate chip cookies and milk. They will need your guidance and help. And they might also need to have their mom or dad as a copilot a few times before they're able to fly solo. Don't be surprised if your child balks the first time he or she has to place a phone call to a teacher or make small talk with your pastor or rabbi. Depending on the circumstances, you might even get some variation of the classic "Mom, you're so embarrassing!" or "Dad, none of my other friends have to do this!"

That's okay. What you'll learn in this chapter will enable you to help your kids work through their "I'm scareds" and "I don't wannas" until they're comfortable. When it comes to teaching kids to connect, remember: It's all about the times at bat. Practice makes perfect—but it takes time. The rewards for your efforts won't be instantaneous. Gradually, though, your children will become more comfortable handling difficult situations the right way. The behaviors you've been modeling and teaching will become instinctual, and your kids will take the lead on their own.

Ultimately, giving your children the tools to connect is as important as—if not more so than—the music lessons you pay for and the sports teams that rule your household schedule. Why? Quite simply, you will have given your children an invaluable tool for success in the real world. A "connector kid" can hold his or her own with adults, stand out in a crowd, and get things done.

Read on for a sampling of scenarios that are ideal for teaching kids to confidently connect every day. This list is not exhaustive—there are any number of situations in a given day that can be used as great teaching tools for your kids. It is meant to be used as a guide to help you to begin to see the world around you with different eyes—so that you can begin to make the world around you a learning lab—and begin to cultivate kids who connect with confidence.

SECTION 1—Specific Scenarios

Eating out. Staying at a hotel on vacation. Making appointments with doctors and hairdressers. Ordering a pizza. Sure, they're all very ordinary activities, and most of us don't give them a second thought. However, they're all "learning lab" moments that parents can use to teach their children important lessons about connecting.

In this section, you'll learn exactly how you can guide your children through navigating a variety of everyday connecting opportunities, as well as why these lessons will benefit your kids for the rest of their lives.

Model Mindfully!

As you begin to model behaviors to your children, consider who is best suited to each type of communication: you or your spouse? The fact is, we all have our strengths and weaknesses. For example, if you are firm and decisive when dealing with service calls from utility companies (and your spouse is timid), you would be best suited to model to your child how to politely deal with solicitors.

Oh, and if you do lose your temper or react in a negative way in any connecting situation, make sure to acknowledge that to your child and explain how you should have acted differently.

The Learning Lab Lesson # 1: Placing a Restaurant Order

"I'll take a hamburger, well done, with pickles on the side, please." Have your child order his own meals and navigate any and all communication with waitstaff. Guide him through getting all the details right (and getting them right the first time), and make sure he is respectful while he interacts. And if the order comes back wrong, guide him through (politely) explaining the discrepancy and getting the problem corrected. Most of the time, kids will enjoy the opportunity to feel grown-up and have control over their meal choice, so this is a casual, no-pressure scenario to get their feet wet in the "connecting" world.

Words to Connect By: If the order is incorrect, your child may need a little guidance on what to say. Make sure he understands how to be polite when explaining the problem, and instruct him to always *request*, not *demand*. Suggest he say something along the lines of:

"Excuse me, I'm sorry to bother you, but I asked for French fries and got a baked potato instead. Is it possible to get them switched out, please?"

Also, be sure to follow up any exchange—including a simple drink refill—with "Thank you so much! This is perfect!" or "Thanks for your help; the food is great!"

The Takeaway: Placing an order at a restaurant is a great way to help kids manage the task of communicating several specific details (dressing on the side, hamburger cooked medium well, or extra pickles, please!) at one time. It's important that YOU, the customer, get them right so that you're easier to work with. All transactions go more smoothly when people like you.

This scenario will also teach children how to be respectful when they are in a position to give direction to someone else. Just because you are the customer, you don't have a right to be rude or condescending. Finally, if you can connect with those who are working for you or with you, you'll get better end results—like a quick resolution to any problems and maybe even extra cherries on your sundae!

Bonus: When the meal is over, if the service was exceptional, have your child approach the manager to thank her for a job well done. You might even ask if you can go back into the kitchen to compliment the chef for a fantastic meal. Remember, kids can have a tendency to clam up in unfamiliar situations, so talk through what he might say beforehand.

The Learning Lab Lesson # 2: Checking in at a Hotel

"I'd like a room with a view!" Traveling outside your personal comfort zone and depending on strangers to meet your needs can be stressful, yes…but it also can be a great learning experience for kids. When you arrive at your destination, have your child do the check-in. Instruct her beforehand on any details she needs to make sure are correct (e.g., non-smoking room, first floor, double beds, etc.).

Words to Connect By: Instruct your child to give the desk attendant all of the information she has upfront instead of waiting to be prompted for answers. A helpful introduction might be:

"Hi, I'd like to check in, please. The reservation is under Smith, and I have my printed confirmation right here."

After the reservation has been confirmed, your child might also say, "Can you check to make sure the room is non-smoking and on the first floor? We'd love to be close to the pool if that's possible!"

The Takeaway: This scenario is a great way for kids to learn the importance of managing details. It's also a prime situation for learning how to ask for things you want, like a certain view or room layout, and how being a connector can get you much further in influencing situations to your benefit.

Bonus: In the event that you find you need something from the front desk like more towels, a replacement for the toothbrush you forgot to pack, or a roll-away bed, have your child place the call to ask for the item.

The Learning Lab Lesson # 3: Calling in Sick

"I won't be at school today, I'm sick!" When kids aren't feeling well and have to miss school, make it their job to gather assignments and work out a makeup schedule with their teachers. And if they aren't in bed with the flu (i.e., too sick to call), have them place the call to the office to say they will be absent. Of course, you'll need to conclude the call in order to confirm that your child is, indeed, not well enough to attend class.

Words to Connect By: Depending on how much work and how many days of school he has missed, your child might feel overwhelmed when he has both makeup work and regular homework on his plate. If this is the case, suggest he ask his teacher for more time—within reason, of course!

"Mrs. Smith, thank you for giving me the chance to make up the work I missed while I was sick. I want to make sure that I understand everything our class went over and that I do my homework well. May I have one more night to complete the assignments you gave me?"

The Takeaway: It's inevitable that every person will have to call in sick at some point in their adult working lives, so there's no better time than the present to help kids learn how to navigate this often-stressful circumstance. (And experiencing the complexities of negotiating a makeup schedule will help them to learn when it's worth laying out and when it isn't!) Figuring out a homework makeup schedule is also a great chance for children to learn how much more willing people will be to work with you when you've connected with them and proven you are both responsible and easy to work with.

The Learning Lab Lesson # 4: The Customer Service Desk

"I need to exchange this shirt. It's a size too small." Whether it's a duplicate birthday gift or a shirt in an incorrect size or a toy that was damaged in its packaging, making returns can be a hassle and, often, an unpleasant experience. Between frazzled employees, long lines, and tricky return policies, making a return or an exchange can be a great chance for kids to truly learn how to "catch more flies with honey than with vinegar."

Words to Connect By: If you're dealing with a particularly frazzled employee, then letting them know that you are sympathetic to their stress from the get-go can change the entire face of your conversation. Instruct your child to lead off with a sympathetic comment instead of a demand for help; for example:

"Busy day, huh? I bet you're exhausted!" or

"Wow, it's really busy in here today. I'm sure you're ready to take a break!"

It might also be the case that the customer—your child—is "in the wrong," so to speak. Encourage her to admit her fault while still politely advocating for herself.

"I know that we're a little late on the return policy, but is there anything you can do to help me? What's the best we can do here?"

The Takeaway: If you've ever fought the return lines after Christmas (or any time, for that matter!), then you know store employees can be less than pleasant to deal with. And if you don't have a receipt or are outside the sixty-day return policy, then it may take some negotiating skills and a lot of patience on your part to get the results you want. In navigating these situations, children will learn the value of being polite, patient, and sympathetic. They will also learn how to negotiate and use what they know (like the details of a store's return policy) to get the results they desire (like their money back!). Finally, those worked-for results (i.e., money in their pockets) will show your children why it's worth taking the time to return merchandise rather than just "letting it go" (and eating the financial loss) because it's too much of a hassle to take something back.

The Learning Lab Lesson # 5: Making an Appointment

"I'd like to make an appointment for…" Between the haircuts, orthodontist appointments, vet visits for Fido, and check-ups at the doctor's office, there are no shortage of opportunities for letting your child fine-tune his phone etiquette and attention-to-detail skills. And if a conflict comes up, have him make the call to cancel the appointment and reschedule it for another day.

Words to Connect By: Explain to your child that it's helpful to him and to the receptionist making the appointment if he has a good idea of what he'd like before beginning the interaction. Instead of an open-ended "I'd like to make an appointment whenever you have one," look at the calendar with him and instruct him to say:

"Hello, my name is [John Smith] and I'm calling to make an appointment for a dental check-up with [Dr. Brown]. Do you have anything available the week of March 12 after 3:30?"

If your child's initial appointment request isn't available, ask him to explain what he wants and to request the next-best option.

"It will have been six months since my last appointment in the middle of March. If it's possible, I'd like to come to your office toward the end of the day so that I don't have to miss school. Can you suggest another appointment that might work?"

Lastly, make sure your child confirms the appointment time to make sure that both parties have the details right.

"Great! So I'll see you and Dr. Brown Thursday, March 22, at 4:15. Thank you!"

The Takeaway: Scheduling an appointment helps kids to learn how to navigate a schedule—both their own and someone else's. Knowing and understanding how much time they need for an allotted appointment or being able to relay all the important details—like the services needed, the type of insurance they carry, or the times that do and do not work—is a great way for them to learn important skills they will need in their adult lives.

Bonus: A big part of being an effective communicator in this respect is making sure you keep the appointments you schedule. Help your kids to keep a calendar—you can print your own off your home computer or set up a dry erase calendar that can be re-used—and assist them in managing the appointments they've scheduled.

The Learning (Lab) Continues!

The everyday situations that you can use to teach your children connecting lessons obviously aren't limited to the five scenarios listed above—but I bet they *have* given you a good idea of how to recognize learning labs and their value to your children.

Here are a few more learning labs to take advantage of—I have no doubt that you can figure out the takeaway, as well as come up with some great words to connect by, on your own!

- **Checking in at Appointments: "Hi, I'm here to see Dr. Jones for an 11:00 appointment."** When you are running around to your various appointments each week, have your kids check in at the front desk. Teaching them to give their name and information, the time of their scheduled appointment, and what they are being seen for allows them to learn how to communicate.

- **Ordering a Pizza: "I'd like to place an order for delivery, please!"** Giving instructions over the phone can be tricky and it's an important skill to master if you want your kids to be connectors. Have them order the Friday-night pizza. Remembering the size, toppings, your address for delivery, along with any other special instructions will give them great practice!

- **Inviting a Friend Over: "Would you like to come play on Friday?"** Asking a friend—or a friend's parent—for a playdate or sleepover is another good opportunity for your kids to work with calendars, make detailed requests, and confirm information. It's also a good opportunity for you to talk to your kids about how to properly handle disappointment when the inevitable rejection is received.

- **Saying "No": "I'm sorry, but I won't be able to come to your party."** Even adults often have trouble saying "no," even when it's in our best interests. By teaching your children to decide when to accept—and not to accept—a commitment or invitation, you'll be doing them a lifelong favor. Make sure you go over polite refusals with them before allowing them to respond. (**Also, po**int out the importance of going to parties and invited activities when appropriate or advantageous, and make sure that your kids thank the host if they are able to attend.)

- **Gathering Constructive Criticism: "What should I work on this week?"** If your children take music or dance lessons, for example, or play on a sports team, make it their job to find out what they should work on before the next lesson or practice. By placing this task—and its execution—in your children's hands, you'll be teaching them a skill that will serve them well with teachers, college professors, and, later, bosses.

- **Filling out Paperwork: "Let's make sure every box has been checked."** While it might not involve verbal communication, teaching your kids to fill out paperwork (or these days, online forms) is still a vital connecting skill for them to learn. Whether they're at the doctor's office, filling out a job application, or applying for a loan, your kids' ability to provide clear, accurate, and adequate information will definitely impact their futures. For now, supervise them as they fill out permission slip forms for school field trips, for example, or ask them to write down their name, address, and phone number at the pediatrician's office. (Be sure to stress the importance of legible penmanship, too!) Your kids will fine-tune their eye for detail, and they'll also feel good about taking ownership of these situations.

SECTION 2—Setting the Scene—Scenarios You Can Create Yourself

Knowing how to recognize and take advantage of everyday connecting learning labs is a great skill for you to have as a parent—but don't think for a second that you need to wait for a "good time" to present itself. You can create plenty of scenarios on your own at any time that will help your kids beef up their ability to connect.

- **Set up a mock interview.** Learning how to present your best self in a short amount of time is all about knowing how to nail a first impression—and that's a valuable connector habit all kids should learn early on. Whether it's a future job or entrance to a school, club, or other organization, it's a sure bet that your child will be faced with an interview at some point. Before she makes it to the interview "big leagues," arrange for her to be interviewed for "smaller" jobs. If, for example, your neighbor wants your daughter to babysit or your great-aunt wonders if she could mow the lawn, ask these adults to first interview their potential worker. Tell them to ask your daughter for her qualifications and experience. Alternatively, you and your child could take turns interviewing one another and then (constructively) critiquing responses.

- **Have your teen get a part-time job.** Working at an afternoon or weekend job has a lot of benefits. But aside from the paycheck and résumé padding, it can also provide invaluable opportunities to build crucial connector skills. Inquiring about available jobs, interviewing, and, eventually, learning to deal with customers and interact with supervisors are all great examples of ways kids can connect at their first job.

- **Encourage them to help elderly neighbors.** When your kids offer to do small jobs for neighbors in need of help, like bringing in their trash cans or newspapers—or simply waving hello—they'll learn to see where help is needed and to respect others, which are major components of connecting.

- **Start a small business.** A lemonade stand, a lawn mowing service, a babysitter—there are plenty of "first jobs" that kids can do, and do well, from a very early age. Learning what it takes to connect with your potential clientele is a great way to get kids started early with learning healthy business habits. Have them create a flier announcing their business and instruct them in introducing themselves door-to-door in the neighborhood to announce their new venture.

- **Teach them how to work their own party.** Unless your kids grow up to be hermits, it will be very helpful if they can learn how to be great hosts or hostesses. When it's time for the next birthday or celebration, allow your child to play an active role in coming up with the guest list. Have him greet all of his friends when they arrive. Then, instruct him to enjoy himself, of course—but also keep an eye open to make sure that everyone feels welcome and included. If gifts are involved, make sure that thank-yous are said, and also ask your child to write more formal thank-you notes to be sent out.

- **Help them connect at the cash register.** If you want good service, you must first be a good customer. Learning the value of connecting with people you do business with— from clients and vendors right down to the lady who checks you out at the grocery store—can mean better experiences for you and for them. The next time you and your kids head out to the market or to the mall, help them figure out how to connect with the people you do business with. Thank an employee who showed you where to find an item, let a manager know about a great service experience, and ask the cashier, for once, how his or her day is going.

- **Ask them to introduce themselves on the playground.** The real world can be a big, scary, and intimidating place. And for kids, the playground is no different. Helping kids to learn how to navigate unfamiliar territory and to make connections with new people is a vital skill that will only benefit them throughout their adult lives. Venture out to a new playground and guide them through making some new friends. On the way, talk through what they might say as they introduce themselves and brainstorm some ice breakers together.

- **Take the dog for a walk.** If you have a dog, taking him for a walk doesn't need to be a solitary activity. Chances are, you'll meet neighbors and other acquaintances while you're out and about. Ask your kids to greet the people you pass, and if appropriate, engage in a bit of small talk. And speaking of neighbors, if a new family moves in nearby, encourage your child to introduce herself to the new kids.

- **Make them do their own fundraising.** If you're like 99 percent of American families, at some point your child is going to have to do some fundraising. Whether it's selling candy for the band, magazine subscriptions for the school as a whole, doughnuts to fund a special trip, or cookies for the Girl Scouts, make your child do the grunt work herself. Too often, parents bring their children's catalogues and sign-up sheets to their offices, ask their colleagues to buy something, and leave it at that. Instead, bring your child to the office for thirty minutes and ask her to do the selling herself! You can also prompt her to hone her saleswoman skills at church, on the phone with friends and relatives, and in your neighborhood. No, you can't expect every child to fall in love with fundraising…but you can expect the experience to boost their confidence, assertiveness, and general conversation skills.

- **Suggest that your kids give a speech.** Encouraging your kids to speak in public from a young age will give them a tremendous leg up on their peers. One of our society's biggest collective fears is public speaking, and it certainly doesn't help that most people have little to no experience speaking in front of a group until it's "crunch time." No wonder we suffer from stage fright! To ease your child into public speaking, first help him brainstorm a subject he feels strongly about—perhaps taking good care of your pets, or what he learned on his recent church trip. Then help him think of an audience who might benefit from this information—maybe a 4-H club, Scout troop, Sunday school class, or service group. Now, you'll need to supervise as he makes inquiries and arrangements to speak, and act as a sounding board as he clarifies his ideas and practices his oration. Yes, this project certainly takes more time and effort than saying hello to a neighbor, but the skills your child develops will be invaluable.

SECTION 3—Connecting the Dots: Life Lessons for Kids Who Will Be Lifelong Connectors

Throughout your life you've learned that there are certain "dos," "don'ts," and "good ideas" in the world of communication. Your parents, teachers, and other mentors shared some of them with you. Others, you had to figure out for yourself—sometimes the hard way. Why not instill as many of these "connecting etiquette" guidelines in your kids as possible before they leave home? The more of these life lessons youngsters learn, the more effective they'll be as they meet new people, navigate various situations, and advocate for themselves.

- **Saying "hello" to important people.** Whether it's the principal at school, the pastor at your church, or the local Scout leader who lives two doors down, it's important for kids to learn the importance of stopping in to say "hi" and the value of forming a positive connection with people—even if it's not someone whom they see as important to their immediate circumstances or well-being.

- **Dealing with conflict issues with a teacher.** Students and teachers don't always see eye-to-eye, and it's tempting to schedule a parent-teacher conference to work out any problems in an adults-only session. But letting your child make the first attempt at smoothing things over with his teacher is a great lesson in connecting, negotiating, and learning to understand another's point of view. After all, a parent-*boss* conference certainly won't be an option later on!

- **Saying they're sorry.** Mistakes happen, and it can be uncomfortable to admit when you're in the wrong. It can also be tempting to place blame and excuse away any wrong-doing. If your family or your child is late to arrive at a commitment, or if she misses an appointment (or if she has misspoken, unintentionally offended someone, forgotten her homework, etc.), have her make the apology. And be sure to let her know that the standard mumbled "I'm sorry" won't cut it. Instead, teach your kids how to genuinely apologize *without* shifting blame or excusing themselves from responsibility. It will make for much better connections.

- **Learning the names of new friends, classmates, and acquaintances.** Explain to your children that they should listen when someone tells them their name—then they should repeat that name and burn it into memory as soon as possible. Also teach them to properly refer to friends' parents by Mr. or Mrs. (last name) rather than (insert friend's name)'s mom—especially when addressing that person directly.

- **Shutting up and listening when having a conversation with others.** Some kids don't listen while "listening" because they're too busy thinking about the next thing they're going to say about themselves when it's their time to talk again. Remind them that it's not always about them and that connecting involves listening and learning more about others. To get started, practice having conversations with your kids and ask them to paraphrase what you've just said.

- **Making it easy for people to do business with you.** When you want something to happen, realize that it will happen a lot faster if you're easy to work with. Explain to your kids that if they want to collaborate with other people, they have to be easy (and pleasant) to work with. Guide them through arranging something—a playdate, a party, or a personal request (like that new bike they want)—and show them how, if they provide all the details, support, and help the person on the other end may need, they will get results much faster!

- **Getting involved.** Make it a rule in your household that each child must be a part of some club, organization, or team—could be anything from Scouts to a religious youth group to a basketball team to a dance troupe. When kids are around others who share common interests, it helps boost their confidence and build friendships, teaching them from an early age how to interact with others. Plus, participating in a regular activity will give your kids opportunity after opportunity to brush up on all of the connecting skills they're learning.

- **Complimenting someone and accepting a compliment.** Compliments can be tricky. You have to know when to compliment someone, and even more so, you have to know how to accept one directed at yourself in a gracious manner. Talk through different compliments and discuss when they are appropriate, when they are too generic, and when they are too grandiose. Likewise, role play with your kids what they should say when someone compliments them.

- **Staying on their best behavior—especially in the presence of adults.** Explain to your kids that even though they may not be directly interacting with an adult, that adult might still be observing and evaluating their behavior. Tell tweens and teens especially that you never know which adult (whether it's a friend's parent, coach, teacher, etc.) might give you (or turn you down for) your first job or write a college recommendation for you.

- **Connecting outside of cliques.** As children get older, the social situations they face become increasingly challenging. As the middle school and high school years become a reality, so does the social pressure of cliques and exclusivity. Teaching kids the importance of making others feel comfortable is a crucial component of connecting. Feeling comfortable enough to approach someone outside of their group and knowing how to make them feel invited and included is something that will benefit your children now AND later in life.

- **Going beyond the "good game."** We tell our kids to be "good sports," and of course we make them shake hands and say "good game" afterwards…but do they *really* understand what it means to be a good sport? Talk about things that your kids can say to their teammates and competitors that will help them to connect better on—and off—the field. Giving encouragement throughout the game (like a "nice shot!" or "way to go!") can make the difference between a forced sentiment and one your children truly mean. Plus, the enthusiasm can be catching for the rest of the team too!

- **Fighting vs. disagreeing.** There's a big difference between fighting and arguing with someone and civilly disagreeing with them. But the lines can easily be blurred for kids, especially when they see their parents veering into hostile territory. Take time to sit down and explain the difference to your children. Work in some tips on conflict resolution and let them see you resolve your own in-house disagreements peacefully.

- **Defusing a bully.** Bullies are an unfortunate reality for many kids, and as much as you'd like to shield your own children from these upsetting peers, that's not always possible—or even advisable. Teaching your kids what to say and *how* to say it in order to diffuse bullying will not only help them to protect themselves, it will also arm them for future scenarios that involve unhappy customers, irate employees, or that furious man you accidentally cut off in the parking lot.

- **Making small talk.** Small talk is an important skill for any connector to have mastered. From the check-out line at the grocery store to the person sitting next to you on your next flight, you just never know when a connection can result in something big for you. When you look at it that way, every connection you *don't* make is another potential opportunity missed. Talk with your kids about arming themselves with five things they can say to connect with people in any scenario. For example:

  1. **Share something extra about themselves.** When adults meet a new child, they'll often ask easy-to-answer stock questions like, "What's your name? How old are you?" In addition to providing the "bare bones" answer, help your children think of something extra they can offer. For instance, your son might say, "Hi, I'm Billy. I'm five years old and I love to play baseball!" Voilà! What might have been a standard teeth-pulling session has just been transformed into a bona fide conversation.

  2. **Be complimentary.** Whether you're seven or seventy-seven, a compliment is always a great way to break the

conversational ice. To get started, teach your kids to comment on something interesting the other person is wearing. For example, "I love that necklace you're wearing. It's so pretty!" Or, "Wow, your shirt is my very favorite color."

3. **Talk about the weather.** Sure, commenting on the weather has a rather "blah" reputation, but the fact is, it works, and it's a great way to ease into a conversation with someone you don't know very well. Teach kids to pay attention to their surroundings so they can comment on them during small talk. For example, "Have you been enjoying the nice weather?" Or, "We could really use some rain!"

4. **Find things in common.** If you can find a common interest with the person to whom you're speaking, small talk can turn from mediocre to meaningful in an instant. Teach your kids to be aware of conversational and external cues. If your daughter notices that someone is wearing a Braves jersey and she's also a fan, she can strike up a conversation about the latest game. Or if your son hears someone say that she's from Columbus, Ohio, he might say, "My grandparents live near Columbus. Don't you love the zoo there?" (Hint: If you are going into a situation and can think of some common interests ahead of time, go ahead and arm your kids with them!)

5. Wrap it up well. One of the trickiest parts of small talk is the conclusion. Give kids a few lines they can use to wrap up a conversation before it veers into awkward silence. "It was great to meet you. I hope to see you again soon!"

- **Mastering the art of saying thank you.** Being a gracious person allows you to connect more easily with others. And saying "thank you," genuinely and appropriately, is the cornerstone of graciousness. Whether it's thanking guests at a birthday party, thanking a sibling for doing something nice, or thanking a teacher for extra help, there are plenty of opportunities in everyday life for your kids to exercise this most important skill.

- **Negotiating.** At some point in their lives, your kids are going to have to negotiate something for themselves. They might be buying a car, asking for a raise, or just haggling over the price of bananas at the farmer's market. Whatever the situation, though, knowing how to negotiate and how to do it well will help them out immensely. For now, take your kids to yard sales and let them talk down the price of a found treasure, or have them negotiate with you on their weekly allowance or weekend bedtime.

- **Remembering the little things.** Often, it's the remembrance of the smallest details that can help us make our most profound connections. Remembering a birthday, a favorite food, or a beloved sports team are great

157

ways to let people know that you are paying attention and to connect with them on a higher level. For example, if you know that your hairstylist mentions how much she loves cupcakes from the bakery down the street, it's a nice idea to take her one when your child's next appointment rolls around. Explain to your kids that making an effort to remember the little things—and acting on them—is a simple way to make a big impact.

> * **Bonus Tip!*** If you're afraid that you won't remember important details for later, it's always a good idea to write them down. Carry a pad of paper and a pencil with you in the car, and take a moment to sit down with your kids in order to record the important details they want to remember for later. If you know you are going to see a particular person again, pull out your sheet of details before your next meeting and talk about ways to use them in conversation.

- **Communicating via social media.** This is something *our* parents didn't have to worry about…but it's essential that you discuss effective and appropriate social media use with your children. Talk to them about privacy settings, what information is okay to share, and how to think about comments and photos. Also, explain to them the dangers of sharing too much with their online friends (or sharing just a little with the wrong people). This discussion doesn't all have to be doom and gloom, though—confirm that social media is a great way to share news and to connect with people you trust.

Tips for Introverted Kids

For some people, connecting with others comes as naturally as breathing. For others, though, introductions, small talk, and being the center of attention are quite difficult. As many as 30 percent of people are introverts, and if your child is one of them, he or she might not enjoy or excel at "being sociable," and may be perceived as shy, timid, or unresponsive. It's important to note that introverts are blessed with their own unique set of strengths, including the ability to be very introspective and insightful, and to connect very strongly with a small group of trusted individuals. Still, though, it's important for your introvert to be able to navigate everyday communications and to be proficient in making necessary connections. Here are some ways to ease your child into connecting scenarios without causing a scene or having a situation end in tears:

- **Manage your expectations.** Whether you're mingling at a neighborhood Christmas party or going to the doctor's office for a check-up, know going in that your child won't be as comfortable interacting with unfamiliar people as her extroverted peers. Enabling her to navigate these situations is probably going to take some work and some time, so remind yourself to be patient and to try not to get frustrated.

- **Take baby steps.** If your child is a fairly inexperienced connector, try not to jump straight into a big scenario like asking him to introduce himself to every long-lost relative at the annual family reunion. Instead, take things S-L-O-W-L-Y and ask him to handle one part of an interaction at a time. To start, introducing himself or answering the "How old are you?" question is great.

- **Try it on family first.** Have kids practice their connecting skills with family or friends with whom they're comfortable before sending them out into the world of strangers. The practice will boost their confidence, and you'll be in a good position to praise and reinforce good communicating behaviors.

- **Arm them with an ice breaker.** If you know that your child is uncomfortable going into a certain situation, give her a few things to say beforehand and practice introductions and icebreakers with her.

The hurdle of the initial connection is often the most difficult for shy youngsters to surmount, so having a game plan in place can help make your child more confident.

- **Stick close.** Introverted kids rely heavily on the support and comfort of having a parent nearby. No, it's not a good idea to allow your child to bury his face in your midriff every time he's uncomfortable in a social situation, and he'll never learn to fend for himself if you answer every question for him. But you *can* stick close by during any interactions and provide encouraging words or help as needed.

- **Follow their lead.** In social situations, pay close attention to your child's behavior and follow her cues. If you prompt your daughter to talk to the waitress when you're eating out and she becomes uncomfortable, for example, don't push too hard. Forcing your child to go past her social comfort zone too quickly will cause her to put up a wall and will make her less willing to participate in the future. Being ready to take up the slack when your child needs help will make you both feel more confident and successful.

- **Set them up for success.** Do whatever you can to set your child up for success in any given scenario. For example, if your child tends to be less comfortable in bigger crowds, try to steer her towards scenarios within the gathering that are more one-on-one. Remember that the more wins your child has, the more confidence he'll build.

Part III

For Kids and Teens from a Teen
—by Lizzie Kuzmeski

8

Communicating with Your Parents: Give Them What They Want So You Get What You Want

I'll start with the bad news: You'll never get *everything* you want. You've probably already figured that out. If your life is anything like mine, you get the occasional "There's no way you're taking the car tonight" or "Under no circumstances do I want you going to that concert" from your parents. (And even though you'd never admit it, sometimes you know they're right.) Plus, we all go to school, to practice, and to family events when we'd really rather be doing something else.

Here's the good news, though—more often than you might think, there *is* a way to get what you want in life and to make sure that other people don't make all of the important decisions for you. One of the best ways, of course, is through good, basic communication. As a teenager, I have learned that kids can have a big influence on what happens in their lives just by communicating effectively with teachers, parents, and other kids. And I promise, knowing that your voice is heard and respected feels GREAT!

Whether you consider yourself to be a natural people person or not, I think that now's the time to learn and practice how to be a good communicator. As a teenager, there are already millions of reasons why knowing how to make a strong, convincing case is a good skill to have. And as we all get older and start to

More often than you might think, there *is* a way to get what you want in life.

take on the world by ourselves, being able to engage effectively with others will help us even more. Before I get into the how-tos, first I'm going to tell you two stories to illustrate how much more effective and efficient good communication is!

Asking, Begging, and Whining May Work, But Not for Long

For as long as I can remember, I've wanted to get a dog. The problem has been that my mom didn't agree, and she had a lot of good reasons why our family didn't need our very own Fido. In order to change her mind I've tried lots of different strategies over the years. For example, when I was about ten years old my best idea was to ask Mom for a dog about ten times a day for six months straight. I also convinced my younger brother, Shane, and my dad to start pleading my case, too.

I guess Mom eventually got tired of hearing "Let's get a dog! Let's get a dog!" over and over, because she finally folded and agreed to welcome a furry friend into our house (but not before asking my brother, dad, and me to draw up a contract specifying who would take care of all the doggie responsibilities, like walking, feeding, brushing, and bathing). Soon Espy, a French Brittany Spaniel, joined the Kuzmeski family.

Before you jump to conclusions, the fact that begging *can* work isn't the lesson in communication I'm trying to share. Actually, applying constant pressure is as likely to backfire as it is to work the way you'd like. (Think about it—for every time begging works, how many more times do your parents tell you not to ask again…or else?) And besides, wearing down someone's resistance is a lot of work for a long time for *you*.

I've found that when you want something—whether it's a dog, help with a big

When you want something your best chance of success is to use smart tactics to get the other person on board.

school project, or a summer job—your best chance of success is to use smart tactics to get the other person on board.

167

The Next Dog—It Was All in the Presentation

A few years after my family got Espy, I found myself in a pet store with my friend and her mother. We began to play with some of the puppies, and (not surprisingly) I immediately fell in love with one that looked just like our Espy. By the time I was on my way home, I was already considering the possibility of getting Espy a friend.

Before long, I asked my unsuspecting mother to go to the pet store to look around. We looked at a lot of animals, including a rare type of turtle and—of course—the puppy I'd seen. Ultimately, though, each critter was much too expensive for my mother to even consider buying on a whim. But the damage was done. I was now hooked on the idea of another dog in the family, and my goal was to get my mom hooked, too.

Unfortunately for me, my parents were not nearly as excited about another dog as I was after I unveiled my big idea to them. I wasn't about to give up easily, but I also knew that I should probably update my persuasion strategy. (No more begging!) After thinking for a few minutes, I went to our computer and started putting together a PowerPoint presentation on why the Kuzmeski family NEEDED another dog.

My first point was that our poor dog, Espy, was getting bored. He needed a friend to be with him when we humans were all away at school and work. He was so bored that sometimes he would sit licking his paws until they were raw and even bleeding. I knew that this behavior made my parents sad, so I devoted several slides to appealing to my parents' love of Espy. I knew that if I could engage their emotions, I'd be a big step closer to getting them to agree with me.

Then I created slides to show why another dog would be a great addition to the family in general, and pointed out how much fun we all could have together. And I included reasons why another dog would not take much more work or money to care for. I even did research on vet and food costs and included the numbers in my presentation.

Finally, I laid out a different option altogether. This option was to get the turtle my mom and I had seen at the store. I knew that this reptile was really expensive and probably less likely to tempt my parents—but it was still another choice for them to consider.

When I showed my parents the PowerPoint after I had finished it several days later, they were shocked that I was able to put together such a nice presentation! They couldn't shoot down my idea without discussion, either, because I had even included a slide rebutting all of the reasons that they might have used to say no. After watching the presentation, my parents found their "no" mindsets changing, and within a few weeks we ended up getting another French Brittany Spaniel named Biscuit! It was all in the presentation.

The Persuasion Breakdown

So now you've seen how much of a difference good communication can make in getting what you want. Granted, not everyone sees getting a dog as life-changing—but I think we can all agree that my well-coordinated persuasion strategy was much more effective and efficient than incessant badgering. And no, I'm not saying that you need to make a PowerPoint presentation every time you want to sway someone to your side of things. I'm just saying that knowing how to connect with others—and why it works—is a skill that will benefit every kid and teen. Following are a few things to keep in mind the next time you're arguing your own case.

It's All in the Details

Before you make your first move—no matter whom you're trying to persuade—do your homework by learning as much as you can about the situation, down to the details. If you've ever taken an algebra class, you know why I'm saying this: When you make a mistake at the beginning of the equation, you'll

Before you make your first move, do your homework by learning as much as you can about the situation, down to the details.

get the answer wrong…even if you took all the right steps afterward. And when you're dealing with people rather than numbers, you'll lose credibility if you get the facts wrong… even though your intentions might be good. So don't make assumptions or rely on what your friend said she heard from her older brother—make sure you have the facts right.

Knowing the details is also helpful because details help you to create a good story. People have told me over the years that I am very observant, and according to my mom specifically, that's one reason why I am able to communicate well. Even as a little girl, I would notice things like the fact that my grandmother had repainted her living room—using the same color of paint—or that the furniture in a room had been rearranged a little bit.

Because I take in details like this, I am able to include them when I write and speak. Sometimes my stories take longer than people like, I think, but it's worth it. The details I am able to give to others help them to understand what I'm talking about and enable me to make my points more clearly. Also, my stories are compelling, and people are more likely to see things from my point of view. My point is, the more details you include, the more people pay attention—and the more likely you are to get what you want.

Including details when interacting with others is also helpful because when you explain things fully and provide relevant information upfront, others don't have to ask you for it. That's important, because being specific and forthcoming helps to ease anxiety and provides credibility. If anything, err on the side of oversharing. (I do!) Being general doesn't give people a compelling reason to see things your way.

Here's an example of how details can work in your favor. Remember my PowerPoint presentation on getting a second dog? I included details I *knew* would tug at my parents' heartstrings, like the fact that Espy was so lonely he licked his paws until they were raw and bleeding. If I had just said, "Espy's lonely," and left it at that, my case would have been easier to ignore because my mom's and dad's emotions wouldn't have been engaged.

Lastly, before I move on to my next persuasion principle, I want to point out that getting into the habit of noticing and sharing details with people to whom they might be relevant can only help you, even when you're not trying to achieve a particular objective. For example, you might think your swim coach doesn't need to know you will be gone over the weekend on a ski trip, but you mention it to her anyway at the end of Tuesday's practice. Turns out, she was thinking about asking your relay team to come in for some extra work on Sunday afternoon. You've just saved her a lot of planning and coordinating that she might have done before calling you later in the week. You just earned yourself some gratitude and respect!

Sell the "Why"

Whether you're trying to convince your friend to come to a party she's on the fence about attending or you're trying to persuade your teacher to give you an extra credit assignment, make an effort to know your audience. This is really important. No matter how much detail you use, you probably won't achieve your objective if your whole argument is self-centered. You need to figure out how your plan or request helps the other person—whether it's your parents, your teacher, or a college admissions recruiter. That's what I mean when I refer to the "why."

The first step in figuring out someone's "why" is to understand and tap into their motivations. What drives them? What are their goals? What would they like to see happen in the future? It's worth taking a little time to figure out what the answers to these questions might be so that you can incorporate them into your case.

> The first step in figuring out someone's "why" is to understand and tap into their motivations.

For example, say that you enjoy playing tennis for fun, and you want to take lessons so that you can really improve and hone your skills. However, tennis lessons aren't free, and the money you have saved from your summer babysitting gig will cover only a few sessions. You can sell your parents on the

173

idea by explaining how important it is to show a commitment to extracurricular activities when you're applying to college (which they're always on your case to get serious about). Your parents will be much more likely to get you lessons if they can see that tennis will be serving a higher purpose than simply entertaining you in the afternoons.

Give It a Positive Spin

Since we were in preschool we've heard sayings like "Always have a positive attitude." And those sayings are good to keep in mind when you are trying to get something you want. When you frame your requests in positive terms instead of negative ones, you will foster the right mindset in your audience. Remember, an upbeat, can-do attitude is more likely to inspire someone's confidence than griping and whining. It's just a matter of making sure your case is half-full instead of half-empty! To show you what I mean, I'll use an example that I'm sure you can relate to: bringing up an academic grade you're not satisfied with.

Say that math is not your strong subject, and even though you're studying and doing your homework, your geometry grade isn't looking so good. You know you need to ask your teacher for some help—and maybe even an opportunity to earn extra credit. Instead of saying, "Mr. Jones, I don't want to fail—can you at least help me to make a C?" (which is negative) say, "Mr. Jones, I think I need some help beyond what I'm doing on my own. What would you suggest I do to improve and become more confident in this subject?" (which is positive). Most teachers (and people in general) will be more willing to help if they see that you are trying to better yourself or the world in some way.

Make It Easy on Them

Okay, so now that you have the details, the "why," and the positive spin, your case needs one more ingredient: your guarantee that you'll be a partner in achieving the outcome you want. When we were little kids, it was fine for us to ask our parents or other authority figures for something and then expect them to make it happen—when you're seven years old, you're *supposed* to let adults take care of the details. But as a teenager, that's not true anymore. You probably won't get what you want if you make a request—no matter how compelling it is—and then completely step out of the picture. If you have the ability to help, you should.

I have noticed (and my mother has confirmed) that people are always more willing to do what you want if you make it easy for them to help and they know they don't have to do all of the grunt work on their own. Tell the other person how you will be involved. Is it possible for you to do research, legwork, or provide support in some other way? Also, it's a good idea to try to anticipate any objections and, if possible, figure out a response.

For example, maybe you want to celebrate your birthday with a party at your house, but you know before you even ask that your parents probably won't be keen on the idea. They'll be picturing hordes of screaming, out-of-control teenagers blaring music and totally trashing their home. You need to show them that you can ensure this apocalyptic vision *doesn't* come to pass.

So first, you tell your parents that you will agree to inviting a certain number of carefully selected friends (to avoid problems) who will leave by 10:30. You'll also throw in $50 for chips and pizza, and you promise not to get orange soda so that if a spill occurs it won't ruin the carpet. Furthermore, you promise to do all the pre- and post-party cleaning. Finally, you tell Mom and Dad that you'll arrange for a carpool so that there won't be a ton of cars parking up your driveway and drawing attention to your house. This way, they'll feel a lot better about agreeing to your party because you'll be taking on a lot of the responsibility yourself!

Set a Good Foundation

If you follow the advice I have given you so far in this chapter, you'll stand the best possible chance of getting what you want. But there are also a few things you can do *all* the time to set a good foundation for yourself. One is behaving and acting responsibly. (Yes, it's okay to roll your eyes. I know I sound like somebody's parent!)

Let's face it, though—adults in general don't always trust teens in general. It's not that they think we're evil... it's more that they question our ability to function alone without guidance. (And honestly, I'm sure we can all identify immature peers who give the rest of us a bad name.) Always try to act respectfully and responsibly and follow through on your commitments so that when you do have a request, adults have a reason to trust you and place their confidence in you.

If you have to start making your case by saying, "I promise, this time is different! I swear I won't flake out!" you're already at a big disadvantage.

Think about this way: If you have to start making your case by saying, "I promise, this time is different! I swear I won't flake out!" you're already at a big disadvantage. (This principle will hold true throughout life with professors, bosses, and more.)

Pick Your Battles

The last piece of keep-in-mind-all-the-time advice I have for you is something you probably won't like: Know when to let it go. I know—nobody likes feeling the sting of defeat, but as the old saying goes, you can't win 'em all. However, if you use your brain, you may be able to influence *which* battles you walk away from victorious.

In my experience, if you've stepped into the other person's shoes enough to figure out the "why," odds are you're familiar enough with him or her to know when you're at the end of the road. Take your parents, for instance—you definitely know the tone of voice and the "look" that they use when you're skating on thin ice. If you see this and still keep angling to get your way until you're shot down—every time—you'll only develop a reputation for yourself as a nuisance who argues for the sake of arguing.

Trust me: It won't always be easy, but be smart and save your battles for things that you *really* want, like changing your curfew—not putting away your laundry or taking out the trash. Also, use common sense and be realistic when planning out your strategy. If your current curfew is 10:00, for example, it's probably hopeless to push for midnight. Start with moving it up to 10:30 or 11:00.

Conclusion

I'm sure you can see why using any—or all—of these strategies will be more effective than whining or arguing or begging. Even if you don't succeed in selling your case sometimes, you'll still have presented yourself as someone who is rational and worthy of respect.

Lastly, I want to point out that all this talk of getting what you want isn't meant to help you manipulate others in a selfish, underhanded kind of way. I just think it's important for people our age to have the tools to advocate for themselves in a way that adults will understand and respond to. Plus, it's good practice. From college professors to bosses to overbearing friends to spouses, there will *always* be people in our lives who will want to tell us what to do and make decisions for us. It's up to each of us as individuals to make sure that we aren't pushed in a direction we don't want to go.

Worksheet: Engaging Adults (and Getting What You Want)

If you'd like, use this worksheet whenever you're laying out a case to get something you want. Filling in each component will help you to cover all of your bases and build the best argument possible.

1. The problem as you see it:

_____

_____

_____

_____

_____

2. The problem as others see it:

_____

_____

_____

_____

_____

3. Why this is a good idea for THEM (not just for you):

_____

_____

_____

_____

4. Solution:

_____

_____

_____

_____

5. All of the objections you can think of (overcome as many as you can):

_____

_____

_____

_____

_____

6. Possible alternatives:

_____

_____

_____

_____

7. Action to take:

_____

_____

_____

_____

9

Creating Better Relationships Means Understanding the Connection

There's a widely accepted stereotype that teenagers are terrible at relationships. According to adults, and to popular culture, people our age are always involved in some kind of drama. Supposedly, we can't make people understand us, we're poor judges of character, and our relationships tend to fall apart at the first sign of conflict. If you don't believe me, just think about how Hollywood portrays it. We've all watched a ton of movies and shows with scenes that go something like this:

PARENT: No! Under no circumstances are you going to be allowed to date that boy! He's trouble.

TEENAGE GIRL: I hate you! You're ruining my life! You totally don't get it!

And then there are the scenes in which someone is double-crossed by a friend. Maybe the stakes are who gets the girl (or guy), or who gets credit for coming up with the solution for a pressing problem. Oh, and don't forget about the plotline that's sparked by a simple misunderstanding—one that could have been easily resolved if the main characters had chosen to have an actual conversation instead of jumping to conclusions.

I could go on with the examples, but I think you get my point: We teens really don't have the best reputation when it comes to being good at relationships. And that's too bad, because I don't know anyone my age who really *wants* to have a negative relationship with their parents, friends, teachers, or coaches. Call me crazy, but I really don't think that we're as bad as pop culture makes us out to be.

Call me crazy, but I really don't think that we're as bad as pop culture makes us out to be.

But maybe there *is* a grain of truth to the stereotypes: We just haven't lived long enough to figure out all the intricacies of good relationships. Sometimes we have to learn lessons the hard way—through experience. Then again, sometimes we don't.

There are a lot of "best practices" you can use to drastically improve almost any relationship. If you let these guidelines influence your behavior, you can prevent a lot of arguments, misunderstandings, and drama, as well as strengthen the connection you have with other people.

Here are some things you can do to create better relationships with just about anyone:

Notice the Little Things

It's the little things that make us who we are as individuals: our mannerisms, habits, and preferences. Your friends might roll their eyes at the fact that you insist on double- and triple-checking the movie time before you all head to the theater, but you know they really don't mind because that little quirk is one of the many things that make you *you*.

It's always a good idea to make an effort to notice these special, unique things about other people in your life. Whether you notice that your friend always orders extra pickles with her burger or your uncle mentions his pet peeve in a conversation, take note of these things and then act on the information. For instance, if your friend is a bit late to dinner, ask for extra pickles when you order for her, and be sure to *always* use a coaster for your drink when you're at your uncle's house!

Noticing the little things and adjusting your behavior to accommodate them will let people know that you mean something to them and that you care. You'll find that they'll probably reciprocate by treating you with more consideration, too! Plus, noticing the little things will strengthen your relationships.

I have seen this principle in action with my best friend, Marissa. (You could also call her my "best connection.")

Recently, Marissa was at my house for a basement sleepover. And the whole time she was visiting, she was asking me questions like, "Lizzie, are you sure you're going to be okay sleeping down here in the basement without a fan? Because I know you can't sleep if it's too quiet." Or, "Lizzie, I know you don't like syrup on your pancakes, so do you just want the butter?"

As Marissa kept asking me question after question, I realized she had remembered everything I had ever told her about me. She had even noticed things I hadn't ever said verbally. In other words, Marissa seems to know me better than I know myself, and this is the reason why she is so important in my life. I love her like she is my sister. It is the understanding, the listening, and the great conversations we have that are the keys to our relationship.

To genuinely connect with someone, you need to make a lasting impression in their minds and in their hearts.

Ultimately, a good relationship is built by giving, listening, and really remembering what a person says to you. To genuinely connect with someone, you need to make a lasting impression in their minds and in their hearts. That is what Marissa has done with me, and I couldn't ask for a better connection or a better friend.

Keep Technology in Its Place

Today, it's easier than ever to create friendships with people. It's an understatement to say that technology is big—everyone is on their cell phones, iPads, computers, and more. Kids are on the Internet more than they are watching TV! Because of these technological devices, most of us have friends we rarely see in person—and may never have met at all (at least face-to-face). I think that's pretty cool—at least on the surface!

In her section of this book, my mom talks a lot about technology. Specifically, she says that because our society relies on it *so much*, it can harm the quality of our connections. She's a big believer in cultivating relationships face-to-face whenever possible. Hopefully you won't think that I'm betraying my fellow teenagers *too* much if I say that to a certain extent I agree with her.

What I mean is, technology isn't evil, but it probably *is* a bad idea to let it define your close relationships. It's important to make sure that our real-life friendships don't accidentally drift into texting-only territory. Here are a few ways to keep technology in its place without banishing it from your life altogether!

First, don't let technology be your only connection in a friendship. Make a point to send an actual birthday card, pop in at a friend's house to say hello, or actually use the phone to chat (instead of texting) if you have a few free minutes. It's hard to pick up on all of those "little things" I mentioned earlier if you're only typing to each other. Plus, I know I feel a lot better and happier after spending an evening with one of my friends than I do after having a texting conversation with her.

If spending time with someone is step one, then being *fully* present is step two. In other words, don't text while you're talking…and maybe even turn your phone to vibrate. On a more basic level, really concentrate on what the other person is saying instead of letting your mind wander or thinking about what you're going to say next. Make eye contact and ask questions to ensure that you really understand what's being said. (My mom calls this "curious listening," and I have to remind myself to do it all the time.)

> If spending time with someone is step one, then being *fully* present is step two.

Being fully present in this way lets people know they're important to you…and it reduces the chances of you missing something important. This might seem radical, but the next time you make plans to spend the night at your friend's house on Friday night, think about putting your phone into your overnight bag while the two of you are hanging out. That way, you won't be tempted to text, check email, etc., and you'll be fully present with your friend. You'll probably find that you're enjoying yourself even more than normal without all of the usual distractions!

Know How to Resolve Conflict

Noticing the little things and keeping technology in its place are two important things for us to remember because they will help us to form and build good relationships. But what about arguments, disagreements, and conflict in general? While the "normal" teenager's life isn't as drama-filled as Hollywood makes it out to be, no relationship is perfect, and we will all face rough patches from time to time.

Conflict resolution is an important skill to have whether you're in an argument with your best friend, having a disagreement with your parents, or at odds with a teacher, just to name a few examples. Here is a good way to approach a heated situation:

- **Make sure you resolve the conflict one-on-one.** …Or with as few people as possible. Bringing in individuals who aren't directly involved is how drama starts! Think about it: You start complaining about your boyfriend's failure to call you last night to all of your girlfriends, and soon they're telling *their* friends, and your gripe gets back to your boyfriend before you have a chance to talk to him. Now you have a lot of damage control to do that wouldn't have existed had you kept your annoyance to yourself. That said, it *is* a good idea to ask a trusted friend or parent for advice if you feel unequipped to handle a situation by yourself!

- **Take time to cool down.** Teenagers are often accused of being ruled by their hormones, and maybe there's a little truth to that. If you feel really angry or upset, wait until you are calmer to approach the other person. Screaming matches and insults might help you to vent, but they won't do much good in the long run. Wait until you're calm, but don't wait until the situation becomes awkward.

- **State the situation as you see it.** When bringing up your grievance, don't start by flinging accusations. Describe the situation as you see it so that the other person understands where you're coming from. I've read that it's good to frame things in terms of your feelings, and doing that has worked really well for me! For example, you might say to your parents, "When you tell me to do something around the house and don't thank me once I've done it, I feel really taken for granted and angry. That's why I slammed my door so hard."

- **Make an effort to understand the other side's perspective.** Realize that it's not all about you. You've had a chance to state your side of the story, so it's important to let the other person do the same. Try to be as calm as you can as you listen.

- **Be honest with yourself.** If you're at fault—even partially—admit it and apologize. If not, try to come up with some way to meet in the middle. The other person will be much more likely to compromise if you are willing to back down first.

- **Think long-term.** Sometimes an honest conversation will end in an apology and a "friends again" conclusion. But not every conflict can be resolved so easily. If you're having trouble coming to an agreement, think about how much the relationship means to you. Would you be okay with not having this person in your life in one month, one year, etc.? Maybe it's worth burying the hatchet...or maybe it's best if you just move on.

- **Always proceed with caution when using technology during a conflict.** If it's good to keep technology from having a starring role in your relationships in general, that is doubly true if you're experiencing conflict. Remember that Facebook statuses, text messages, and emails are forever. Even if you're boiling mad, don't give in to the temptation of Tweeting something nasty about another person!

Here's an example of how all (or at least most) of this might play out in real life. Let's say you are planning on going to the movies with a friend and she cancels at the last minute because she's sick. You end up going with your mom instead, and you see your friend in the lobby of the theater with her new boyfriend. Obviously, you're mad that she canceled your plans and lied to you about the reason why! You stew about her behavior all night long, and several times you contemplate texting her or writing on her Facebook wall to call her out. In the end, though, you decide to wait until you see her at school the next day to talk about what happened.

Finally, lunch rolls around, and you ask your friend (let's call her Kathy) if you can talk to her alone. Then you tell her you saw her at the movie theater last night, and that you felt rejected, hurt, and angry because she blew you off and then lied to you. Then you ask her what happened.

At this point, I hope that Kathy will 'fess up and apologize to you. I think we can all understand being obsessed with a new crush, let alone boyfriend (or girlfriend). Still, you and she both know that that doesn't excuse her behavior, and she promises to be honest with you in the future. Before you go back to class, you make plans to see a different movie—just the two of you—over the weekend.

Of course, it's always possible that Kathy might get defensive or even deny being at the theater with her boyfriend. In this case, there's not a lot you can do other than politely distance yourself from her and hope that she decides to make a move to mend the conflict later.

Strengthen Your Connections:
The Saga Continues!

I think that the three connection principles I have explained in this chapter will help just about anyone improve their relationships. But they certainly aren't the whole story! I have learned enough things from my mom, my friends, my own experiences, and more to fill a whole book, much less a chapter. That said, here are a few more pieces of relationship-building advice that I think we teenagers can really benefit from:

- **Be loyal.** I have alluded to this already but the principle is worth repeating. Don't backstab or gossip. Don't go behind a person's back, even if you don't particularly like him or her. No one will consider you a real friend if they can't trust you.

- **Never lie.** This goes hand-in-hand with being loyal. I know that it can be really, really hard to tell the truth sometimes, but honest relationships are good relationships. Even if you get away with dishonesty at first, it will probably catch up to you eventually— call it karma if you want!

- **Be responsible.** Do what you say you're going to do. People will like you more when they know they can count on you, especially adults! When you prove yourself to be reliable, trustworthy, and a person who does his or her best at all times, others will be more willing to forgive mistakes when they *do* happen, and they'll also be more apt to help you out whenever you need a hand.

- **Be generous.** Being generous doesn't necessarily mean giving away money. (I know—we teens don't often have a lot of it to start with!) You can also be generous with your time, attention, and talents. Look for opportunities to do something selfless "just because." For example, you might offer to give your mom a break and cook dinner, or leave a "You can do it!" note in your friend's locker before a big test. Teens have a reputation for being self-centered, so try to prove it wrong.

- **Always say "thank you."** Gratitude counts. It's important to let others know that you've noticed and are appreciative of what they do for you. Plus, saying "thanks"—for help with homework, for a ride to school, or just being a good friend—helps *you* to realize how fortunate you are.

Creating Better Relationships

Ultimately, building good relationships is a skill. And just like any other skill, practice makes perfect. The more you concentrate on understanding, helping, and engaging with other people, the better you will become at it. Of all the life skills you can concentrate on developing, the art of connection is *definitely* one of the most important.

Worksheet: My Relationships

This worksheet will help you to think about the relationships in your life and to identify ways by which you can make them better.

1. List your best relationships:

_____

_____

_____

_____

2. What does a good relationship mean to you?

_____

_____

_____

_____

3. What do your closest friends do that makes them a valuable part of your life?

_____

_____

_____

_____

_____

4. How can you take the key elements of your best connections (see answer to #3) and spread them to others to make those relationships better?

_____

_____

_____

_____

5. Think of a relationship that you had that ended badly. What lessons did you learn from the experience? Looking back, what do you think you could have done differently?

_____

_____

_____

_____

A Call to Engage: Concluding Thoughts from Maribeth

Thank you for reading *The Engaging Child*. I enjoyed writing this book, especially because I got to work so closely with Lizzie during the process. I treasure the time I get to spend with my daughter and realize that the days I'll have her home with me are numbered. Working on this book together has taught us so much about each other, and for that I am grateful.

Now I'd like to ask *you* a question: Did what you read resonate? I hope so, because I am 100 percent convinced the ability to connect with others and form strong, meaningful relationships is one of the greatest gifts you can give to your kids.

More to the point, I hope you won't say, "Well, that was interesting!" and then put the book down and continue on with your life business as usual. I hope you will take this message to heart. I hope you will resolve to put the tips I shared into practice—starting now and continuing as your child grows.

Connecting skills have always paid off. They've always greased the gears of business and fostered productive relationships both in and out of the workplace. But now, thanks to the double-whammy of globalization and a struggling economy that shows few signs of improvement, the need for those skills has suddenly ratcheted upward.

If you have these skills, you can be (with apologies to Marlon Brando) a contender in the economy of the future. I think that's what all of us want for our children.

Please, please, please invest in helping your kids learn how to engage others. Not only will your efforts pay off in the future, they'll pay off in the present. Before you know it you'll be hearing comments like "What a charming, well-mannered young man!" or "Your daughter is so mature for her age…I know you must be proud!"

In other words, the journey I'm asking you to undertake is a deeply rewarding one. The joy of nurturing a garden doesn't wait to appear when everything is in full flower; it reveals itself as each new sprout appears and each blossom unfolds. As you watch your son or daughter grow more confident and articulate you'll get to celebrate every day. And you'll be astonished as you see positive changes spring up in every area of your child's life.

With parenting, as with most other tasks, where you place your focus is where you see results. Please focus on the skills laid out in this book. Day-to-day life teems with opportunities to help your children hone their connecting and engaging skills. You don't have to seek them out. You just have to pay attention.

Quite simply, raising an engaging child requires engaged parents. Our kids are the future. They deserve nothing less.

Maribeth Kuzmeski
November 2011

About the Authors

Maribeth Kuzmeski, MBA, CSP, is the author of six books including *...And the Clients Went Wild!* and *The Connectors* (Wiley), and is a frequent national media contributor and international speaker. Maribeth and her firm, Red Zone Marketing, Inc., consult and train businesses from financial services firms to Fortune 500 corporations on strategic marketing planning and business growth. She has personally consulted with some of the world's most successful CEOs, entrepreneurs, and professionals. Maribeth lives in the Chicago, IL, area with her husband and two teenagers.

Lizzie Kuzmeski is a teenager and a natural connector. She enjoys theatre, horseback riding, and, yes, Facebook. ☺